European History in Perspective
General Editor: Jeremy Black

Published
Ronald Asch *The Thirty Years' War*
Christopher Bartlett *Peace, War and the European Powers,
1814–1914*
Mark Galeotti *Gorbachev and his Revolution*
J. L. Price *The Dutch Republic in the Seventeenth Century*
Francisco J. Romero-Salvado *Twentieth Century Spain*
Brendan Simms *The Struggle for Mastery in Germany, 1779–1850*
David Sturdy *Louis XIV*
Peter Waldron *The End of Imperial Russia, 1855–1917*

Forthcoming
Nigel Aston *Frederick the Great*
Nigel Aston *The French Revolution*
N. J. Atkin *The Fifth French Republic*
Ross Balzaretti *Medieval Italy: A Cultural History*
Robert Bireley *The Counter Reformation*
Donna Bohanan *Crown and Nobility in Early Modern France*
Robin Brown *Warfare in Twentieth Century Europe*
Patricia Clavin *The Great Depression, 1929–39*
Geoff Cubitt *Politics in France, 1814–1876*
John Foot *The Creation of Modern Italy*
Alexander Grab *Napoleon and the Transformation of Europe*
O. P. Grell *The European Reformation*
Nicholas Henshall *The Zenith of Absolute Monarchy, 1650–1750*
Colin Imber *The Ottoman Empire, 1300–1481*
Brian Jenkins *European Nationalism*
Martin Johnson *The Dreyfus Affair*
Trevor Johnston *International Relations in Europe, 1492–1715*
Timothy Kirk *Nazi Germany*
Peter Linehan *Medieval Spain, 589–1492*
Marisa Linton *The Causes of the French Revolution*
Simon Lloyd *The Crusading Movement*
William S. Maltby *The Reign of Charles V*
David Moon *Peter the Great's Russia*

(List continues overleaf)

Peter Musgrave *The Early Modern European Economy*
Kevin Passmore *The French Third Republic, 1870–1940*
Roger Price *1848: A Year of Revolution*
Maria Quine *A Social History of Fascist Italy*
Martyn Rady *The Habsburg Monarchy, 1848–1918*
Tim Rees *Rethinking Modern Europe: A Rural Perspective, 1750–2000*
Richard Sakwa *Twentieth Century Russia*
Thomas J. Schaeper *The Enlightenment*
Graeme Small *Later Medieval France*
Hunt Tooley *The Western Front*
Peter G. Wallace *The Long European Reformation*
Patrick Williams *Philip II*
Peter Wilson *From Reich to Revolution: Germany, 1600–1806*

THE DUTCH REPUBLIC IN THE SEVENTEENTH CENTURY

J. L. Price

Senior Lecturer of History
University of Hull

St. Martin's Press
New York

THE DUTCH REPUBLIC IN THE SEVENTEENTH CENTURY
Copyright © 1998 by J. L. Price

St. Martin's Press, Scholarly and Reference Division,
175 Fifth Avenue, New York, N.Y. 10010

First published in the United States of America in 1998

This book is printed on paper suitable for recycling and
made from fully managed and sustained forest sources.

Printed in Hong Kong

ISBN 0–312–21732–3 clothbound
ISBN 0–312–21733–1 paperback

Library of Congress Cataloging-in-Publication Data
Price, J. L.
The Dutch republic in the seventeenth century / J. L. Price.
p.   cm. — (European history in perspective)
Includes bibliographical references and index.
ISBN 0–312–21732–3 (cloth). — ISBN 0–312–21733–1 (pbk.)
1. Netherlands—Civilization—17th century.   2. Netherlands–
–History—1648–1714.   3. Netherlands—Economic conditions.
I. Title.   II. Series.
DJ156.P75   1998
949.2'04—dc21   98–24084
                                                      CIP

CONTENTS

Preface   vii

Map: *The Dutch Republic in the Seventeenth Century*   ix

Introduction   1

1 The Impact of a New State in Europe   16

2 The Economic Miracle – and its Limitations   39

3 Republicanism in Practice   61

4 Religion, Politics and Toleration   86

5 A Bourgeois Society?   108

6 A Divided Culture   129

Notes and References   152

Glossary   163

Further Reading   165

Index   168

PREFACE

In writing a work of this sort an author inevitably relies more on the work of other historians than he or she can easily acknowledge. In my own case, I am somewhat uncomfortably aware of the extent to which my understanding of almost all aspects of Dutch history has been built on the foundations laid by others. However, a full scholarly apparatus and comprehensive bibliography would be out of place in this introductory work, and I have kept the notes to a minimum and restricted the references in Further Reading to the most useful and accessible books and articles in English. This practice, although justifiable, does no justice to my scholarly debts. Perhaps I can restrict myself here to expressing my gratitude to Professor E.H. Kossmann, whose teaching first introduced me to the history of the Dutch Republic and who guided my first tentative steps in historical research, and let that stand as a substitute for a longer list of acknowledgements which would be unavoidably arbitrary and necessarily incomplete.

One person who deserves to be singled out for thanks is my friend and colleague Louis Billington, who read the penultimate version of the book in full and made a number of both acute and useful comments. I acted on most but, perhaps unfortunately, not all of his recommendations.

This also seems a good opportunity to register my appreciation for the generations of students in the History department at the University of Hull who have responded to my attempts to teach them about the Dutch Republic with patience and good humour. I have learnt a lot from having to try to make myself clear to students for whom the subject was almost invariably completely new; my own experience suggests that undergraduate teaching is a valuable discipline for the academic, and one which is now becoming sadly underrated.

Recent years have been particularly stressful at British universities for a variety of reasons; and my sincere thanks for helping me to retain my sanity in these unpleasant circumstances go to Michael, Jonathan and, not least, Cassie.

Hull
13 January 1998

The Dutch Republic in the Seventeenth Century
(Reproduced from J. L. Price, *Culture and Society in the Dutch Republic during the Seventeenth Century* (1974) by permission of B. T. Batsford Ltd)

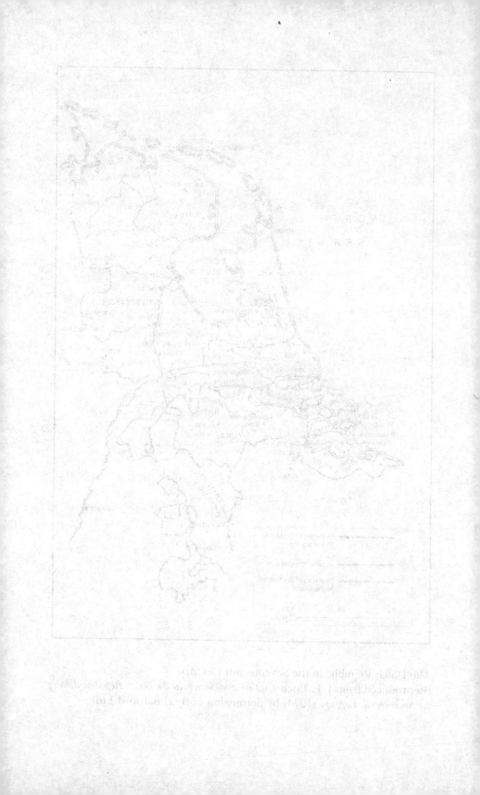

INTRODUCTION

The new state which emerged from the Revolt of the Netherlands appears at first glance to be a somewhat haphazard collection of territories thrown together by the accidents of rebellion and war. In the aftermath of the break-up of the short-lived united Kingdom of the Netherlands and the creation of a separate Belgian state after the revolution of 1830, both Dutch and Belgian nationalist historians tried to discover an historical necessity in the existence of two separate states in the Low Countries. Consequently they argued that the earlier division between North and South brought about by the Revolt was similarly the result of fundamental differences not historical accident.[1] Later generations of historians have found it rather more difficult to believe that the Dutch and Belgian peoples were already in existence in some sense before the Revolt, and that this national divide determined the political outcome of the movement. As far as the Dutch Republic is concerned, while it may be possible to discern long-term similarities in the social, economic and cultural developments of its constituent provinces, what is more immediately evident is the lack of much natural unity among them. In particular, the actual extent and boundaries of the new state seem more obviously the result of geo-strategic forces than of historical inevitability.[2] The more defensible areas north of the great rivers survived to become the core of the new state, and the eventual border between North and South was determined by the course of the war with Spain. Rather than the Dutch people creating the Dutch state, the Dutch state created the Dutch nation.

Until the risings in the towns of Holland and Zeeland in 1572, the centre of resistance to the policies of the Spanish government in the Netherlands had lain in the south rather than the north; and the Pacification of Ghent in 1576 seemed to unite the Habsburg Netherlands as a whole against Spain. However, this fragile unity collapsed

1

within a few years, and most of the south either returned to obedience to Philip II or was conquered by the Spanish army. The Union of Utrecht (1579) eventually included the seven most northerly provinces, but most of the towns of Flanders and Brabant which had joined the Union were brought back under Spanish control by the army of the prince of Parma during the 1580s, and Brabant withdrew from the States General of the Union for this reason in 1585. This loss to the Revolt of the two historically most important provinces of the Netherlands thus seems to have been largely the result of military factors: they could not be defended effectively against the Spanish army, while the more northerly provinces were both further away from the starting point of the Spanish reconquest and also able to utilise the defensive possibilities offered by the great rivers.

Had this been the whole story, however, it is unlikely that the northern provinces could have held out for long. One reason why they were in fact able to survive was the diversion of Spanish efforts, first into the Armada against England, and then into the invasion of France in support of the Catholic League from 1589 onwards. However, the political and economic strength of the province of Holland, which formed the core round which the new state could develop, was of at least equal importance. In the crucial period between the mid 1580s and the virtual establishment of Dutch independence in the truce with Spain of 1609, many of the rebel provinces were able to contribute little to the common cause because of the devastating effects of the war – fought to a large extent on their territory in these years – so Holland's political leadership and, especially, Holland's taxes were even more important for the Republic in this period than they were to be in the mature state. This province was able to take the lead so effectively because both its political cohesion and its fiscal system had developed considerably in the decades before the Revolt. The States of Holland had gained considerable experience of floating loans on the credit of the province, and of collecting taxes to support them. This fiscal experience, administrative autonomy and consequent increased responsibilities provided a sound foundation for effective political action in the years after the rising of 1572.[3] Holland's economy was able to withstand the disruptions to trade, manufactures and agriculture brought by the Revolt and resume its remarkable rate of growth by the 1590s, and this economic strength meant that it could provide the resources which were needed for a successful prosecution of the war against Spain. The peculiar importance of the province of Holland for the Republic as a whole in this period was more of a strength than a weakness for the new state, but was not without its problems even then.

It was not easy to create an effective state out of the rather fortuitous assembly of rebel provinces brought together under the Union of Utrecht. The differences between them in history, size and economic development were considerable, and even the common interest in defence against the Spanish army could not always disguise the existence of distinct and possibly conflicting political agendas. A far-reaching particularism allied with mutual lack of trust threatened for some years to destroy the new polity before it had been given the chance to establish itself properly. A fundamental problem was that there was no historically nurtured unity between these particular provinces: although the Burgundians and later the Habsburgs had brought most of the Netherlands together under their rule for a large part of the north this was a very recent development. Utrecht, Overijssel, Friesland and Groningen had only been incorporated into the Habsburg Netherlands in the 1520s, and Gelderland as late as 1543 after a prolonged period of hostility to the policies of Charles V in the region. Thus the northern provinces had had only a very limited experience of living together within the same political community, and this brief period was hardly sufficient to wipe out entirely the legacy of a history in which conflict figured rather more prominently than peaceful coexistence. Indeed, within the Netherlands as a whole north/south contacts and sympathies – for example between Holland and Zeeland and Flanders and Brabant – were probably distinctly stronger than those between the maritime and the inland areas of the north.

This lack of any historically nourished community between the various provinces making up the Union was exacerbated by very real differences, or even conflicts, of interests over a whole range of issues. These were to some extent overridden or masked by the immediate demands of the war, but remained a potential impediment to wholehearted cooperation. Indeed, the very diverse ways in which military operations affected different provinces contributed to a mutual distrust. From the time of the Pacification of Ghent (1576), Holland had been almost completely free of enemy troops and had seen virtually no acts of war within its boundaries; in contrast, Spanish troops were able to occupy the town of Groningen in 1580 and, especially after the fall of Antwerp in 1585, for the following two decades the war was mostly fought out in an arc of territory from

Friesland in the north to Gelderland and the remnant of Brabant still in Dutch hands in the south. This sharp contrast in the experience of the reality of war was a constant source of friction between the relatively favoured Holland and Zeeland and the provinces whose towns were constantly threatened with occupation or siege, and whose countryside was regularly devastated or laid under contribution by enemy troops. Moreover, interprovincial quarrels were joined by conflicts within the provinces themselves to make the development of a common policy and political purpose yet more problematic. Quite apart from the deep divisions which were stirred up by the earl of Leicester's unfortunate period as governor-general, it was often difficult to reach a consensus over crucial issues even within Holland itself. The particularism which made cooperation between the provinces so difficult could also weaken their internal political coherence.

A central issue, perhaps even the most important motivation, of the Revolt was the protection and preservation of the 'privileges', the traditional rights of individuals and groups, against what was seen as the absolutist and centralising policies of the Spanish government in the Netherlands.[4] In consequence, the inviolability of the political rights, not only of provinces but also of privileged towns and nobilities within the individual provinces, became a fundamental constitutional principle of the new state. In this conception of politics, a town represented in the States of Holland, for example, could no more be forced to accept a policy it opposed than Holland itself could be constrained to bow to a majority in the States General of the Union. In these circumstances, the problem facing the political élite was to find a way of getting the political system to work while going with the grain of particularism: those local and provincial freedoms which the Revolt had been fought to preserve had not only to be respected, but had to be the defining characteristic of the new polity.

This insistence on local and provincial autonomy was exacerbated by the disparity in size and wealth between Holland and the other provinces. The fact that the province of Holland contained almost half the total population and over half the total wealth of the Republic was to be a permanent problem for the Dutch political system, but it was especially obvious and divisive in the period before 1609 during which the land provinces were so disrupted by war while Holland remained relatively untouched. Holland needed to be reassured that it could not be forced to follow policies it opposed simply at the behest of the other provinces – whose financial contribution to the common cause, even taken together, was far less than its own at this time. The smaller provinces, in contrast, required a way of preventing the dominant province from riding roughshod over what they saw as their interests. In the end it proved possible to devise a political system which could meet such apparently contradictory requirements more or less satisfactorily, but it is hardly surprising that it took some time before this could be achieved, and that the result bore the marks of its makeshift origins.

The religious situation in the provinces which made up the Union was also a source of instability. The Revolt had produced *de facto* religious pluralism while the conventional wisdom of the time asserted that unity of religion was essential to the stability of the state. In addition, although the Revolt was far from being simply a protestant uprising against intolerant catholic rule, the Reformed Church had emerged from the years of strife as the dominant church despite its membership remaining relatively low until well into the seventeenth century. In contrast, the catholics almost certainly remained the largest single religious grouping during much of this period but had been deprived of the right to the public exercise of their faith, and the property of their church had been confiscated. An inadvertent pluralism combined with an official church with a minority following does not seem to be a likely recipe for religious peace, but in the event this situation proved far less unstable than might have been expected. As we shall see, religious divisions did lead to a major political crisis in the early seventeenth century, but its origins lay in disputes within the Reformed Church and not in animosity between protestants and catholics as might have been expected. The reformed[5] movement managed to win for itself a privileged position within the rebel polity in the years immediately after 1572; yet it represented only a small proportion of the population as a whole at this time, and even among the political élite its support was uncertain. Of course, in religious matters at this time it was not absolute numbers that mattered, but the degree of commitment and political influence of its adherents, yet its distinctly low membership constituted a problem, and one that was perhaps as much political as religious. However, support for the church was probably not as weak as has often been supposed as, besides those who formally became members, there was a category of people who were regular attenders at services but not (yet) members. The former can, in principle though not always in practice, be counted but how many of the latter there were can only be guessed at. So the often-quoted contemporary estimate that only 10 per cent of the population were members of the Reformed Church in the middle of the 1580s, while a forceful reminder of the numerical weakness of the new church, should not be treated as gospel. So the Reformed Church became the official church – though not the state church, as there was no duty of membership or even of attendance at its services – but this position gave the political authorities considerable leverage over it. Right from the beginning there was an uneasy relationship between the new church and the civil power,[6] but a certain identification of the Reformed Church with the Dutch state and its political élite was established at an early stage. The civil authorities at local, urban and provincial level recognised and supported the church, and slowly the expectation developed that the regents – the political élite – at all levels would be members of the Reformed Church. This understanding was important in itself even though, or perhaps especially because, the practice lagged well behind the theory; catholics, dissenting protestants, and lukewarm supporters of the Reformed Church remained an important element in the regent group as a whole, at least until the political crisis of 1618 gave a decisive boost to religious orthodoxy.

The presence within the Republic of protestants who were not members of the Reformed Church, nor particularly sympathetic to it, was an important factor influencing the attitude of the regents in religious matters. Most important numerically at this time were the anabaptists, in particular the various groups of mennonites,[7] who had managed to shake off much of the stigma of their earlier reputation for violence, and were coming to be seen as peaceful and hard-working. At a time when the Reformed Church was trying to embrace a larger proportion of the Dutch population, and was in consequence in danger of being seen as diluting the demands it made on its members, the high moral standards and strict congregational discipline of the mennonites made them an attractive alternative to many. However, it was probably precisely this austerity, together with an incurable tendency to split up into quarrelling subgroups, which in the long term led to their numerical decline. Perhaps less numerous but probably more influential politically were those who regarded themselves as protestant but who were neither dogmatically inclined nor firmly attached to any church or sect. Such ecumenical or erasmian protestants were well represented among the better educated, and their ideas were influential among the political élite for pragmatic as well as for idealisic reasons; a relatively tolerant approach to the confused religious situation of the time seemed to make good sense, as well as being probably more congenial to many regents. Such attitudes were reinforced by an ill-defined but pervasive anticlericalism or, put more precisely, a general determination among the regents that they would not allow their policies in religious matters to be dictated to them by the Reformed Church.

However, it was the persistence of traditional religious beliefs and practices in the Republic which made the situation so unclear and made the regents determined to stick by their pragmatic policies. Catholics, in one sense or another, probably made up a majority of the Dutch population until well into the seventeenth century, but there is a danger of exaggerating both their numbers and their religious consciousness. It is all too easy to count committed protestants and to assume that all the rest were catholics in some significant sense, while ignoring the large but ill-defined and uncountable group of those who were in favour of some sort of reform within the church but who were not yet clear how far it should go, not to mention the possibly even larger group of those who were religiously indifferent, or had become so during the upheavals of the Revolt. Ecclesiastical discipline and pastoral care had broken down with the defeat of the old church, and the Reformed Church was unable, and perhaps to an extent unwilling, to take over its responsibility for the whole population. The flight of many catholic priests and the difficulty of finding any, let alone any adequate, protestant replacements meant for many a significant break in communal religious experience, and at least some may well have welcomed the relaxation of religious pressure and surveillance.

The religious beliefs, attitudes and perceptions of much of the Dutch population are even more problematic: they may well have been more catholic than anything else, but that is not necessarily saying a great deal. At the time of the Revolt the church in the Netherlands had been still essentially untouched by the Counter-Reformation, and the catholic laity were in the main ill-prepared to sustain a clear perception of the essentials of their faith in the uncertain years that were to follow. Before the coming of the mission priests, the attitude of this quasi-catholic section of the population was possibly more clear in its negative response to protestantism than in any positive affirmation of the values and beliefs of the old church.

If the political and religious spheres were marked by uncertainty in the early years of the new state, the economic situation can be seen in retrospect in a more positive light. Although the economy of the northern provinces had undoubtedly suffered from the disturbances of the early years of the Revolt, by the late 1580s it had picked up momentum again and was well on the way to the decisive breakthrough to European, if not world, dominance.[8] This was part of a much longer chain of causation: the basis of the Dutch economic miracle of the seventeenth century had already been laid before the Revolt and, indeed, it is hard to conceive of the Revolt itself succeeding in the way that it did if the economy of the province of Holland in particular had not been so strong. The boom of the last years of the century[9] was only possible because of the developments in economy and society in the earlier years of the sixteenth century, if not before.

In particular, the expansion of Dutch trade was foreshadowed by the success of the trading activities of the maritime provinces of the northern Netherlands in the late fifteenth and early sixteenth centuries. It was in these years that the merchants and seamen of Holland and Zeeland in particular began to dominate trade to the Baltic, and notably to control the shipping of grain from the Baltic region to the growing population of western and southern Europe. This trade, together with other so-called 'bulk' trades, was the most important single element in later Dutch commercial success, and its basis was clearly formed in these years. More generally, not only was this commerce directed by merchants from the maritime provinces, but the goods concerned were carried in ships built and owned in, and manned by seamen from, this region.

Manufactures and the fishing industry were also well established in the maritime provinces by the middle of the sixteenth century. Admittedly, the textile industry, centred particularly on Leiden and Haarlem, was somewhat ailing and needed the boost which immigration and the associated introduction of new techniques brought at the end of the century, but the towns – at least in Holland – were beginning to grow rapidly. The fishing sector was becoming a major source of both employment and profit, particularly as the fishermen from the northern provinces began to dominate the lucrative herring fishery. Indeed, along with the grain trade, the herring fisheries of the North Sea were to be one of the main foundations of Dutch economic success. In turn the expansion of Dutch shipping and fisheries proved to be a stimulus to the development of shipbuilding together with its associated activities. The shipyards of the region proved able to respond positively to the opportunities presented, and not only produced more vessels but began to design and build specialised bulk carriers and fishing boats. However, the chief locus of most of these developments was the maritime region, and most particularly Holland; the economic imbalance between the maritime and the land provinces which was to be so characteristic of the seventeenth-century economy had its roots in this earlier period of economic growth.

At least as important a part of the rapid development of the economy of the northern provinces before the Revolt was the beginning of the transformation of the agricultural sector which was to be an indispensable part of later Dutch success.[10] Essentially, what was beginning to develop, particularly in the western areas, was a market-oriented farming sector thoroughly integrated into the trading system of the region. The import of Baltic grain helped to free the agricultural sector from the need to produce bread grains on land which was not especially suitable for this purpose, and allow it to concentrate on more suitable and lucrative specialised areas such as dairy-farming, the fattening of beef calves, and market-gardening to serve the growing population of the towns. In return, the rural sector became an important market for grain and for whatever else it was no longer producing itself, and in addition stimulated the growth of an artisanal service sector in the small towns and villages of the region to supply its other needs.

Social and economic change in the countryside was inextricably linked to the development of the urban sector. Here the province of Holland at least was startlingly different from the rest of Europe even before the Revolt. In a Europe where the vast majority of the population lived and worked in the countryside, it has been estimated that in Holland about half the population lived in towns by the middle of the sixteenth century.[11] Outside Holland the forces of commercial capitalism were also bringing about fundamental changes – though not at the pace, nor necessarily in the same direction as in the leading province. As with the economy, rather different societies were emerging in the advanced western and in the inland regions, a contrast that would be a prominent characteristic of the Dutch economy in the following century.

The world seemed a dangerous place for the Republic in its early years: the war with Spain continued until 1609, and even then was interrupted by a truce, not a peace, and effective allies in this struggle were hard to find and even harder to keep. Even through the fog of hindsight it is easy to understand why a decisive Dutch defeat was regarded as a distinct possibility throughout the 1580s, and only a remarkable political and military consolidation in the following decade ended the immediate threat of annihilation. France and England were the obvious potential allies for the Dutch against Spain for strategic and religious reasons, but Elizabeth was reluctant to get involved – and England had probably neither the money nor the military strength to intervene effectively in any case – while the continuation of the wars of religion hamstrung successive French kings and made a pragmatic approach to foreign policy almost impossible. In the end, the fall of Antwerp in 1585 induced England to come to the aid of the Dutch, but this help proved less effective than might have been hoped. More decisive was the inadvertent French assistance: it was the diversion of the Spanish armies under Parma to aid the Catholic League against the new – and for a while protestant – French king Henry IV that gave the Dutch the breathing space from Spanish pressure that they needed.

Despite the Spanish monarchy's position as a world power of apparently unassailable strength, the multifarious demands on its resources and the strain of almost uninterrupted warfare meant that it was much weaker in practice than it seemed to contemporaries. Under Philip II and his son, the empire included Spain, its possessions in Italy and the Netherlands in Europe, and its immense colonial territories in central and southern America and the Philippines, together with Portugal and its colonial possessions in Brazil and Asia. In addition to the sheer size of the empire ruled by the Spanish kings, what seemed to make the *monarchía* especially formidable was the flow of precious metals, especially silver, from Mexico and Peru to fund its war effort. Yet each possession of the Spanish crown seemed to cost more to administer and, particularly, to defend than it brought in revenue, and Spain's world-wide empire inevitably involved similarly world-wide commitments. In the Mediterranean, Spain faced the formidable threat of the Ottoman empire, in western Europe the latent rivalry, not to say hostility, of France, and in the Caribbean the constant depredations of English and other pirates and privateers. On top of all this, the constant drain of the campaign against the rebels in the Netherlands, and especially of maintaining the large army this required brought the Spanish fiscal system near to collapse.

In contrast, the Dutch had a meagre territorial base by almost any standards and their cause seemed doomed while the Spanish army under Parma made slow but apparently inexorable progress, coming to a climax with the taking of Antwerp in 1585. Yet they had some advantages which made their position less desperate than it appeared on the surface. First of all, they had no distractions; all the resources that the rebels were able to muster could be concentrated on the fight for survival against Spain. Secondly, as the Spanish army moved into the northern Netherlands it began to meet conditions which, given the military technology of the time, were considerably more favourable to the Dutch. The defensive possibilities offered by the great rivers, and the ability of the Dutch to operate on internal lines in this area – while the Spanish had to use more clumsy external lines – suggest that, even if the Spanish effort had continued without diversion, it would still have faced a considerably more formidable task in the north than it had had to deal with in the south. Most importantly, if the Dutch could hold out long enough, the strength of their economy would begin to tell in terms of revenue and the military resources that it could support. In the long term, if there was a long term, the Dutch would win.

That there was a long term for the Republic was first of all a result of the international situation and the way Spain chose to react to it. For a complex of reasons, not all of them clear, Philip II diverted his resources and, despite Parma's protests, those of the army of Flanders first to the Armada campaign against England, and then to large-scale intervention in the civil wars in France in the hope of preventing Henry IV from establishing himself on the throne. As far as the Netherlands was concerned, these decisions forced Parma to halt his brilliantly successful campaign against the rebels, and go on the defensive in the north. This relieved the Dutch of immediate Spanish pressure and gave them a prolonged breathing space, which has been seen by many historians as vital for the survival of the Revolt. Yet such a respite on its own was not enough to save the nascent state; the outcome depended on how well it was used. The emergence of Johan van Old-enbarnevelt as the effective political leader of the Republic began to bring some purpose and consistency to a foreign policy which had been singularly lacking in these qualities since the death of William the Silent (1584). Although formally only *Advocaat van den Lande*[12] of Holland, Oldenbarnevelt was able to bring policy under his control and establish his command of international politics with remarkable speed. Within less than a decade he had secured the effective recognition of Dutch independence by England and France, and had transformed the Republic into an equal, and indeed formidable, player in the game of international politics. By the time France made peace with Spain in 1598 and, less significantly, England also withdrew from the war against Spain after the accession of James I (1603), not only was the diplomatic position of the Republic strengthened and clarified, but Spain under a new king had clearly shot its bolt and was unable to make much progress despite its ability for once to concentrate on the struggle in the Netherlands. The strains of long years of warfare on a country which was essentially poor were finally beginning to be unmistakable.

Behind these external successes lay a remarkable transformation of the internal situation in the new state. Most fundamental was the creation of a political system which worked despite the formidable problems outlined above; this remarkable achievement, together with the related organisation of an effective fiscal system which provided the necessary support for the Republic's armed forces, was to a significant extent the work of the indefatigable Oldenbarnevelt. The latter had made his political mark as *pensionaris*[13] of Rotterdam, and the post from which he dominated the Republic for over thirty years was advocate to the States of Holland, thus very much a provincial office. This provincial base of his power made it perhaps less surprising that the political system he established went with rather than against the grain of particularism, and he used the principle of provincial autonomy to ensure Holland's leadership in the new polity. As Holland was effectively in control of Dutch policy, it was prepared to use its burgeoning prosperity to pay for it; in consequence, it proved possible to find the financial resources to support the military effort the Republic needed to survive. Without this sound fiscal base the military reforms of this period would not have been possible. As it was, the joint achievement of count Maurits and his cousin, Willem Lodewijk, was to push through military reforms which created perhaps the most modern and effective army of the time, and one which was large enough not only to prevent any further Spanish successes but to establish control over the core territory of the Republic. A flexible and powerful naval force was also essential: logistical and tactical support was needed for the army, convoys had to be provided for the protection of trade, and both a battle fleet and ships to blockade the Flemish ports were required: the results were perhaps less spectacular, and less noticed by historians, but were nevertheless no less impressive and just as necessary as the achievements of the army.

By the time of the truce with Spain in 1609, it is clear that pragmatic solutions to the difficulties outlined above had been found, but equally it can be said that in the main these were ways of living with the problems, not of solving them. The underlying situation remained essentially unchanged and it remained to be seen if the compromises which had been arrived at would hold for any length of time.

In politics, a way of running the polity had been found which worked despite its theoretical insufficiencies. However, the political situation was still volatile, and only after surviving the crisis which erupted during the Truce could the system be said to have bedded down. The relationship between the state and provincial autonomy was unclear, and the related question of sovereignty within the Republic was equally opaque, and it was not clear how they could be lived with; in the end these and other uncertainties became permanent features of the republican system,[14] but with conflict over the nature of the Reformed Church linking with disputes over foreign policy in the first decade of the new century, it was far from clear at this point that the system could take the strain.

As far as religion was concerned, pluralism was more or less firmly established, though its modalities remained flexible, but major trouble was looming within the official church. The conflict between the self-styled orthodox and a more liberal wing over the teachings of the Reformed Church was also linked to the uncertain relationship between the church and the civil power, as the remonstrants not only offered the prospect of an official church on a broad reformed base, but also of one which was prepared to recognise unequivocally the authority of the magistrate in ecclesiastical affairs.[15] What made such uncertainties and disagreements particularly explosive was the unsettled nature of the religious allegiances of much of the population: the protestant message was still in the process of being spread, and many areas of the country were as yet little affected, while conversely the Catholic Church was only just beginning to organise its missionary effort effectively. Both the paranoia of the calvinists and the desire of many regents to make the official church more broadly attractive are understandable in this labile situation.

In general it can be suggested that the identity of the new state – and of its inhabitants – was as yet problematic. The Republic had been created from seven of the seventeen Habsburg provinces, but what were its proper boundaries? It already controlled substantial parts of Brabant: should its ultimate aim be the liberation of the whole of the south, or was this already a pious dream rather than an outcome any practical politician either aimed for or desired? In the end the Dutch could only be defined as the inhabitants of the new Dutch state, but until its borders were stabilised no one could be sure just who these were, or ought to be. Such uncertainties were exacerbated by the disagreements over foreign policy which arose during the peace negotiations which preceded the truce of 1609. In particular, the political leaders of Holland, with their eyes firmly on the economic interests of their province, favoured peace, while the land provinces were less attracted to a policy which might expose them to danger in the future.

Such differences of political perception between the provinces were reinforced by the rapid economic growth and social change of the early decades of the seventeenth century. The province of Holland was the centre of this development with the other provinces lagging more or less far behind. The jealousies as well as the practical divergences of interest which arose out of such changes made cooperation between the united provinces more difficult yet. Nevertheless the Dutch Republic was to become a successful polity with a booming economy and flourishing cultural life – and by the end of the seventeenth century it was at least somewhat clearer who and what the Dutch were.

The amount of material available in English on the history of the Dutch Republic has improved considerably in recent years, but many gaps still remain. One of them is the lack of a succinct survey of the present state of historical research on the seventeenth century. Israel's recent book[16] covers more than three centuries, and is perhaps on rather too large a scale to be ideal as an introduction, while the section of Geyl's work covering the seventeenth century[17] is now more than half a century old and, moreover, is marred as a study of Dutch history by his insistence on dealing with North and South together. Haley's brief survey[18] is still useful, but much has happened in Dutch historiography since its publication. The present book is intended to provide an introduction to the major themes of Dutch seventeenth-century history and to give the reader a taste of recent developments and debates in the historiography of the period – though flavoured throughout with the author's own interpretations. The first chapter looks at the problems facing the new state as it emerged into a world that was dangerous for the Dutch but yet also offered them considerable opportunities, not least that of becoming a major power in Europe, and perhaps the world. They were able to take on this role because of the strength of their economy and the nature of Dutch economic success is dealt with in the following chapter. Chapter 3 is concerned with the peculiar political system of the new state and argues that it worked well in practice despite contemporary and later criticism. The problems, not least political, caused by the religious pluralism of the Republic and the circumstances which not only gave rise to toleration but also limited its scope are the themes of

Chapter 4. The final two chapters are concerned with the peculiar society and culture that emerged in the Republic at this time, and discuss the extent to which they constituted something new in the social and cultural history of Europe. Although there is an unavoidable arbitrariness in the order in which the topics have been dealt with, the one chosen makes sense to the author and it is to be hoped that in the end the reader will agree.

1

THE IMPACT OF A NEW STATE IN EUROPE

The Dutch Republic was a new state in early seventeenth-century Europe and yet it rose to the position of a major power within only a few decades of its uncertain emergence into independence. Precisely when the Republic can be said to have become an independent state is difficult to say. It could be traced to the risings in the towns of Holland and Zeeland in the summer of 1572, but until the Pacification of Ghent in 1576 they were just a handful of rebellious towns with a very uncertain future, and after this agreement they were a part of a wider political constellation comprising almost the whole of the Habsburg Netherlands but with an almost equally uncertain status. The traditional starting point for the Republic is the signing of the Union of Utrecht in 1579, although this was an alliance for the better prosecution of the war with Spain and not the conscious founding of a new state. Perhaps the rejection in 1585 by Henri III of France and Elizabeth of England respectively of separate offers of sovereignty over the rebel provinces could be marked as the point at which the Dutch decided they had to go it alone, were it not for confusion of their status which resulted from the ambiguities of the governor-generalship of the earl of Leicester. Only after Leicester's ignominious withdrawal from the Netherlands in 1588 can the Dutch Republic be seen as entering into European history as a fully independent actor. Yet within a decade of this point, the Dutch situation had been transformed: while under Leicester they had remained under heavy military pressure from the Spanish, and appeared on the edge of defeat,[1] by the time Philip II of Spain died in 1598 the Republic under Oldenbarnevelt was not only reasonably secure from military defeat, but was beginning to negotiate on almost equal terms with the leading European powers. The climax to this phase of the emergence of the Dutch state came with the negotiations with Spain and signing of the truce in 1609 which signalled, implicitly at least, Spanish acceptance of Dutch independence.

The emergence of a new state in Europe was an unusual phenomenon in this period; the Dutch Republic was the only unambiguous case in the whole of the early modern era. Sweden had broken away from the union with Denmark/Norway in the early sixteenth century, but this was simply the re-emergence of a kingdom which had previously existed. Similarly, Portugal asserted its independence after the revolt of 1640, but had only been dynastically linked with Spain since 1580, so this again was the reassertion of an already well-defined separate statehood rather than the emergence of something new. Perhaps the nearest equivalent to the Dutch case is the rise of the Swiss Confederation in the late middle ages. By the early sixteenth century the Swiss cantons were effectively independent, but their rise had been slow, and their impact on the rest of Europe was distinctly limited – though Zürich and Geneva in particular had a significant influence on the development of the Reformation, and Swiss military innovations made an important contribution to the transformation of military practice in Europe in the fifteenth and early sixteenth centuries.

If the fact of the emergence of a totally new state in Europe was unusual, the speed with which the Republic was able to achieve the status of a major power was even more out of the ordinary. Again there were some near parallel cases of minor powers rising quite suddenly to prominence, but nothing quite as dramatic as that of the Dutch. After regaining its independence, Sweden enjoyed a century of decent obscurity until it emerged dramatically under the leadership of Gustavus Adolphus as the champion of protestantism in the Thirty Years War. It was to retain – though sometimes precariously – the status of a major power for the rest of the century, but a series of defeats in the early eighteenth century returned the country to the minor status from which it had sprung. In contrast, the startling speed of the rise of the Spanish monarchy to quasi-hegemonic status in the sixteenth century receives less attention than perhaps it deserves. Even after being united through the dynastic link forged by Ferdinand and Isabella, Castile and Aragon can be seen as no more than minor powers at the beginning of this century, yet when the abdication of Charles V brought to an end the union of all Habsburg lands with the imperial title, the Spanish *monarchía* was suddenly revealed as the greatest power in Europe, with the possible exception of the Ottoman empire, with seemingly inexhaustible riches flowing in from the Americas to fuel its pretensions. In this case, too, the period of greatness was relatively short; already by 1640 the combination of the Portuguese breakaway with the revolt of Catalonia marked its end, though the extent of Spanish weakness was not fully apparent till the 1660s and the sick man of Europe was resuscitated to a certain extent in the following century.

The parallels both in extent and in timing between the rise and decline of Spain and the similar course of the Dutch Republic are superficially intriguing, but perhaps no more than that. The foundations of the *monarchía* were the well-established kingdoms of Castile and Aragon while the Dutch state was an entirely new creation with no discernible historical roots. Also Spanish power owed much to dynastic accident, and it took much of the first half of the sixteenth century before its potential, supported by a flow of precious metals from the Americas, could be fully realised. In contrast the Dutch Republic arose out of rebellion and war, and within a few decades was firmly established among the states of Europe and was also a major military and naval power. Comparisons can only make the unique quality of these developments more evident.

In a number of ways the Dutch state was an anomaly in the Europe of the seventeenth century: it was a republic in an age of increasing absolutism; it was held together by a minimal state and radically decentralised at a time when growing state power has been seen as the norm; and, perhaps most surprising of all, it tried to follow secular priorities in a Europe riven by religious disputes, and to pursue peaceful trade in an era of vicious great power rivalries. Yet the underlying paradox of the Dutch Republic is that this apparently peaceful trading society was born in armed rebellion, established its independence in a war against Spain which lasted (nominally at least) 80 years, and was more often at war than not until the treaty of Utrecht (1713) ushered an unprecedented period of peace in the early eighteenth century. Indeed, the Dutch state was a response to the needs of war and remained almost wholly dedicated to the organisation and financing of war:[2] without the need for a common defence and military policy it is doubtful whether the Dutch provinces would have ever come together to form a joint polity.

However, the concentration of the central institutions of the Dutch state on war and the preparation for war does not mean that Dutch professions of their peaceful aims were hypocritical: on the contrary, one characteristic that distinguished the Dutch from almost all the rest of Europe was their lack of territorial ambitions – at least within Europe. Whereas foreign policy was conventionally seen in terms of honour, and success measured very largely by territorial gains, the Dutch had to a significant extent moved outside this set of perceptions and values. Apart from the preservation of their own independence, they saw foreign policy in terms of the pursuit of material, and particularly economic, advantages and not of the honour or glory prescribed by the values of a noble culture. To this extent the Dutch Republic represented a cultural revolution in perceptions of the nature and purpose of international relations, distinguished not by machiavellian amorality – which was all too common at the time – but by a change in the ends which were to be so ruthlessly pursued.

Of course, the simple statement of lack of territorial ambition requires some qualification. The attitude of the Dutch towards the southern Netherlands remains a problem. On the one hand the idea of the unity of the Netherlands as a whole retained some influence until well into the seventeenth century, while on the other it can be argued that it had already disappeared as a practical object of Dutch policy before the end of the sixteenth century. Certainly, as late as 1630 there were hopes that a rising in the south could be exploited to drive the Spanish out and achieve some sort of unity for the Netherlands as a whole; yet at the same time the modest conquests that were in fact being made in Brabant and Limburg were revealing the problems involved in ruling populations which were by this time firmly catholic. Moreover, the merchants of Amsterdam and of Holland in general were not eager for a 'liberation' for the south which might release Antwerp from the shackles of the Dutch blockade of the Schelde and allow it to compete with them on equal terms. Very practical considerations undermined the hopes of religious and political liberation for the south, and the absorption of all or part of the southern Netherlands faded from the realm of practical politics until the early nineteenth century.

The peaceful image of the Dutch also needs to be modified in the light of their aggressive support of their economic interests and, in particular, by the violence which was an inevitable part of their colonial expansion in this period. In Europe they were ready to use armed force, or the threat of it, to protect or promote their trading interests, as is shown by their use of their naval strength to intervene in the conflicts between Sweden and Denmark in the 1640s and 1650s in order to achieve and maintain a favoured status in relation to the Sound Toll.[3] Less dramatically, their blockade of the Schelde which continued even after the end of the Eighty Years War in order to restrain Antwerp's trade, although it could be justified on legal grounds, was maintained by force. Holland in particular regarded a large navy for the protection of trade as essential, and this defensive role could often appear rather threatening to others. The naval blockade of the Flemish ports during the war with Spain provides another example of the use of Dutch navy in ways which could be seen as rather less than pacific by those affected; notably, Dutch attempts to enforce the embargoes decreed by the States General on neutral shipping were, to say the least, assertive.[4] Opportunities for using the Dutch army to support Dutch economic interests were much more limited, but the Republic's neighbours were frequently made aware that it was prepared to back its strategic interests with military force. An early example of this was the Dutch response to the tangled affair of the Jülich–Kleve succession (1609–14): as Spanish troops moved into two of the disputed territories, so Dutch troops occupied the other two, and to the inhabitants there must have seemed little difference between the aggressive Spanish and the defensive Dutch. In general, Dutch policy was to maintain a screen of strongpoints protecting the Republic's eastern border, and it is unlikely that this could have been achieved without a certain amount of coercion. Such transgressions against a purely pacific policy can be justified as primarily defensive in nature, and were minor matters in any case compared to the massive and consistent use of force in the building-up of the Dutch trading empire. Although Dutch aims were primarily economic, at least in the East – the situation in the Americas was rather more complicated – whenever it was necessary to use force in the pursuit of these objectives they did not hesitate. Their position in Java and the Moluccas – the spice islands – was not built up solely by trading skills and the exploitation of economic advantages but also by coercion. Local rulers were pressured into contracts and treaties which were favourable to the Dutch by the threat or even the use of force, and military and naval action was needed to take over forts, factories and trade from the Portuguese. Dutch ruthlessness was shown at its least humane in the policies which were adopted to limit and control clove production in the Moluccas: force was used to end the growing of cloves in the North Moluccas and to limit their production elsewhere so that the VOC[5] could establish a

monopoly. The lure of nutmeg similarly led the Dutch to quasi-geno-
cide on the Banda Islands.[6] In the end the pursuit of profit in the East
drew the VOC into establishing territorial control over much of Java
and Sri Lanka by the end of the seventeenth century, but these colonies
were not the result of any particularly powerful imperial impulse but
came as by-products of commercially motivated policies.

The Dutch record in the Americas is less clear cut. Here the West
India Company was divided in its objectives between profit, and attacking what were seen as the colonial roots of Spanish power. Thus the
attack on Portuguese Brazil – which was a part of the Spanish empire
until the Portuguese revolt of 1640 – was an extension of the Eighty
Years War as much as an attempt to gain control of Brazilian sugar
production. The WIC turned its attention to Brazil soon after its
foundation in 1621, and in the 1630s and early 1640s it seemed on
the verge of significant success, but the Republic lacked the will to give
the WIC effective support, particularly after the Portuguese revolt
deprived the campaign of strategic significance for the Dutch struggle
with Spain. Other major aspects of the WIC's activities – privateering
and the slave-trade – show little evidence of pacific leanings where
profit was in prospect.

The republican character of the Dutch political system, and its radical
decentralisation, is much less ambivalent. In an age when both monarchical rule and a strong central government were seen as essential to the
survival of states, the Dutch rejected both and prospered – at least for a
while. However, it can be argued that the worst effects of a republican
system were counteracted by the power and authority of the princes of
Orange, who provided leadership and unity that would otherwise have
been fatally lacking. The role of the princes in the Dutch political system
will be discussed more fully later,[7] here it needs only to be pointed out
that for long periods of the seventeenth century they did not in fact play
this part and the Republic did not collapse. Until 1618 Maurits was
largely confined to a military role and the Republic was led by Oldenbarnevelt and Holland, and from 1650 to 1672 Willem III was largely
excluded from political life, so for 40 years of the century the house of
Orange was in no position to play the unifying role which has been
imputed to it. So, although under the leadership of, successively, Maurits,
Frederik Hendrik and Willem II in the period from 1618 to 1650, and
then Willem III from 1672 onwards, the political system was in practice
something of a hybrid, for the rest of the century it was purely republican
both in form and in practice.

The very limited powers exercised by the central government also marked the Republic off both from conventional thinking about the nature of the successful state and from the centralising tendencies of the time. Here again it can be argued that the authority wielded by successive princes of Orange gave greater power to the centre in practice than the formal system seemed to allow, but this is only a part of the explanation as to why the system worked. More importantly, acceptance of provincial – and even subprovincial – autonomy was a recognition of the realities of political power in the Republic and enabled the very disparate elements composing the Republic to come together on a minimal programme of joint action. Within this system, the wealth of Holland enabled it to play a dominant role in defence and foreign policy without threatening the autonomy of the other provinces. Paradoxically, it was the principle of provincial autonomy which allowed Holland to dominate, and it was very largely the leadership given by this province which provided the Republic with relatively consistent and effective policies throughout the century. In other words, the Dutch Republic succeeded because of, not despite, the extent of its local and provincial autonomy.[8]

The Dutch state was involved in warfare for much of the seventeenth century despite the desire of the regents who controlled its politics to be allowed to pursue their economic ends in peace. Certain elements in the State – most notably the princes of Orange and their supporters – may have had other priorities, and so turned less reluctantly to war, but their political influence is not the explanation for the Republic's continual involvement in armed conflict. The Dutch were at war so often in this period because for much of the time they had no realistic alternative: they found that either their continued existence as an independent state or their vital interests were threatened by the power of Spain, the envy of England or, later, the aggression of France, and they were forced to defend themselves. The world into which the Republic was born was a dangerous place, particularly for a protestant state dependent on trade.

In the first place, there was the continuation of the Eighty Years War which lasted until 1648, interrupted only by the Twelve Years Truce of 1609–21 (which, surprisingly, lasted its full term). Although it can be argued that the Republic had effectively won its independence by 1609, this was not finally recognised by Spain until 1648 and the existence of the new state and the extent of its territory remained the fundamental issue of the war until the end. However, neither the course nor the outcome of this war can be properly understood without taking its context into account. The Dutch war with Spain can be seen as part of a broader European struggle against Habsburg hegemony which had its origins in the early sixteenth century. The Thirty Years War was in the end a decisive phase in this conflict, and was also linked to the religious struggle of the time between an increasingly militant and confident catholicism and a protestantism driven, at least in its own eyes, onto the defensive. A notable aspect of these conflicts is the way that they spilled out over the confines of Europe into Asia and the Americas, though perhaps to talk of world wars[9] is something of an exaggeration. The failure to crush the Dutch Revolt was the first intimation that the power of the Spanish *monarchía* was not what it seemed. On the surface this was more than impressive: in Europe the Spanish kings controlled Naples and Sicily, Milan, and in effect much of Italy, while Franche-Comté and the Netherlands gave them a firm base in northern Europe; outside Europe, Mexico and Peru were the core of the most impressive colonial empire of the age; while from 1580 onwards Portugal and its trading empire in Asia were added to this agglomeration of territories. It is hardly surprising that contemporary states feared for their survival when faced with such a power, especially when it was bolstered by a great and regular flow of silver from the Americas. In practice, however, the Dutch were able to hang on and begin to draw in the help of other powers which also felt threatened by Spain. In one of its important aspects, the Hispano-Dutch war was thus the arena in which Spanish hegemonic ambitions were fought and defeated, and the enormous strain of this long struggle must be seen as one of the chief explanations for the decline of Spain as a great power by the middle of the seventeenth century. This long-term drain on Spanish resources had already done much of its work when the Dutch alliance with the French in 1635 initiated the final and decisive phase. The Treaty of Münster which brought the Eighty Years War to an end with the confirmation of Dutch independence also marked the end of Spain's era of greatness. Although it was able to regain Catalonia – though not Portugal – and carry the war with France to an honourable conclusion (1660), its underlying weakness became clear to the rest of Europe by the 1660s when it proved unable from its own resources to defend the Spanish Netherlands from French aggression in the War of Devolution (1666–67).

Although the Dutch were always anxious to avoid direct involvement, the final decades of their struggle with Spain were also inextricably linked with the Thirty Years War. The Bohemian revolt against (Austrian) Habsburg rule which sparked off the conflict was reminiscent in many ways of the Dutch Revolt, particularly in its defence of traditional political rights against the encroachments of absolutist government, and of protestantism against repressive catholicism. More compelling for the Dutch, however, was the danger that a decisive victory for the imperial side in the Holy Roman Empire would undermine their own position. The Spanish-Imperial plan in the middle of the 1620s to conquer a Baltic port and set up an admiralty with the specific intention of destroying that pillar of the Dutch economy, the Baltic trade, shows how closely the two conflicts were linked in the minds of contemporaries.[10] Consequently, the Dutch were in effect involved in the Thirty Years War from the outset, attempting to organise support for the Bohemian rebels and subsequently for the other opponents of the Habsburgs in the Empire. The intimate relationship between the two conflicts is symbolised by the fact that the treaty of peace between the Dutch and Spain was signed as part of the wider Peace of Westphalia which finally brought the Thirty Years War to an end.

The long struggle against Spain was also in part an expression of that religious conflict which clearly played so important a role in the history of the period, and yet is still extremely difficult to evaluate. The degree to which the Revolt was essentially a protestant rising and the Republic a protestant state can both be debated, but what cannot be doubted is that the survival of the rebellion was a defeat for catholicism, and that the new Dutch state at the very least would never be a champion of resurgent counter-reformation catholicism. More positively, the Dutch victory over Habsburg Spain ensured the survival, and indeed dominance, of protestantism in their country, and the Dutch state was the focus of protestant hopes and fears for much of the first half of the century. Here again the Eighty Years War links into the Thirty Years War which similarly, while not being simply a religious conflict, had profound religious implications: a victory for the Austrian Habsburg emperor might not have signalled the total eclipse of protestantism in the Empire, but the history of the Bohemian lands warns us not to underestimate either the power or the ruthlessness of triumphalist catholicism in this period.[11]

However, the support given by catholic France both to the Dutch and to the protestant side in the Empire is a pertinent reminder that these were never simply religious conflicts, and that reason of state could and did cut across confessional loyalties.[12] Perhaps the strongest effect of the religious divide on European politics was the degree of distrust and paranoia which it induced. Both catholics and protestants were vulnerable to rumours of international conspiracies by the other side, and protestants believed that the papacy had absolved catholics from keeping their treaty obligations where these clashed with the interests of the Church. For all the divisions within the protestant camp, and despite the fundamental conflicts of interest between the leading catholic powers, polarising tendencies in religious terms were very strong in the early seventeenth century. In the case of the Dutch, such perceptions went with the grain of their central political objective: the aim of establishing their independence from Spain was strengthened by the awareness of what defeat would mean for protestantism. Victory for Spain would bring the triumph of intolerant catholicism and a renewal of persecution, and probably of a greater intensity and effectiveness than anything the Netherlands had experienced in the previous century. Similarly, they feared that a catholic victory in the Empire would inevitably be followed by an attack, inspired more by religious than geo-political motives, on the Republic. To an extent, the Dutch, whatever the strength of the pragmatic element in their foreign policy, were trapped in the protestant camp.

They were also assigned the role of champion of European protestantism by contemporaries on both sides of the religious divide. This was partly out of choice, or at least expedience. Ever since the beginning of the Revolt the Dutch had sought help and allies where they could find them, and appeals to protestant solidarity had been their stock-in-trade as far as the German protestant princes and England were concerned. Alongside the perception that the struggle against Habsburg hegemony was being fought in the Netherlands came the parallel idea that Reformation and Counter-Reformation too were fighting it out here, and even when the latter struggle shifted more obviously to the Holy Roman Empire, the Dutch involvement remained obvious to all.[13] Although happy to use such perspectives when it suited them, the leading Dutch politicians were in the main pragmatic not so much from inclination as necessity; the young state needed catholic help from the start, and an alliance with catholic France remained a cornerstone of Dutch foreign policy, even if this meant neglecting the interests of French protestants. Indeed, this aspect of policy could be difficult to explain, and Oldenbarnevelt's attempts to keep on good terms with France after the death of Henry IV could be put in a most suspect light in the context of the religious disputes within the Republic at the time.[14] Even in this period the pragmatic and the confessional interpretation of the Dutch position in Europe did not necessarily coexist without contradictions.

In the early decades of the century – and in this case hardly interrupted even by the Twelve Years Truce of 1609 – the conflict with Spain extended its range outside Europe. In retrospect, much of this seems of relatively minor significance: the outcome of the war was not decided in the Americas or Indonesia. Also the Dutch would have attacked the Portuguese position in the East even if Portugal and its empire had not been absorbed by the Spanish. However, such colonial conflicts were influenced by the struggle in Europe and, indirectly at least, the course of the latter may well have been affected by events outside Europe. Although the hopes of the founders of the West India Company that it could decisively weaken Spain by attacking its American empire may have proved to be vain, the Dutch attack on Brazil together with their success in undermining the Portuguese position in the East may well have contributed to Portuguese discontent with Spanish rule. Certainly the Portuguese revolt of 1640 was one of the chief reasons why Spain finally decided to cut its losses and make peace with the Dutch on almost any terms. Dutch colonial activity in the first half of the century was not just an offshoot of the Eighty Years War – the VOC's campaign in the East had its own logic and momentum, and the attempt to take control of part of Brazil continued after Portugal's break with Spain– but the WIC was set up, at least in part, to weaken the Spanish by attacking their position in the Americas,[15] and in effect the war was fought not only in Europe but also in the Americas and the Far East.

After the final settlement with Spain in 1648, Dutch hopes for peace were first disappointed by successive wars with England. These were fought primarily at sea, and were a threat to Dutch trade and prosperity rather than to their survival or independence. On land they remained largely undisturbed, though the invasion by the troops of the bishop of Münster during the Second Anglo-Dutch War constituted rather more than an irritation. The Dutch trading economy had been able to expand during the war with Spain, but even in this case the damage inflicted on its shipping and fishing fleet, notably by Dunkirk privateers, was far from negligible;[16] during the sea wars with England the disruption was much greater. The sheer size and ubiquity of the Dutch merchant fleet made it vulnerable to attack and very difficult for the Dutch navy to defend, and large numbers of Dutch vessels were captured during these wars. Insurance charges on ships and cargoes rocketed, trade was held up, and in some years the herring fleet was unable to sail. There were also knock-on consequences for employment in the trading towns, and even in the manufacturing centres which were largely dependent on seaborne trade to find markets for their products. There was also an extra-European dimension to the wars with England: colonial rivalries – and especially English resentment at Dutch success – were important in creating a climate which made these conflicts possible, and it is wholly appropriate that the second war began with a clash of rival fleets off West Africa, and ended with an exchange of colonial territories.[17]

As damaging as the wars with England were to the Dutch economy, they were overshadowed from 1672 onwards by the emergence of France as a threat to the very existence of the Republic. The combined attack by France and England on both land and sea in this year seemed at first to have been fatal, with French troops sweeping across the land provinces and reaching the border of Holland by the early summer. However, the Dutch navy held off the combined French and English fleets, and the inundations of the 'water-line' defences checked the French, and allowed the Dutch to regroup their forces. The experience had been traumatic, however, and for the rest of the century the Dutch would be either at war with France or preparing for it. The near-disaster of 1672 brought Willem III to power in the Republic, and for the rest of his life he was the chief organiser and animator of a series of coalitions designed to check the perceived threat of French hegemony. In a reversal of the situation in the first half of the century, in these years the Dutch looked to the Habsburgs – though in this case chiefly the Austrian branch, as the weakness of the Spanish had already become unmistakable during the War of Devolution – for help against France. England played an ambivalent role, being seen by the Dutch, or at least by Willem III, as a natural ally in the struggle with France, but under Charles II and James II in fact pursuing policies which were at least as likely to favour the French as to oppose them. Eventually the Dutch invasion of England in 1688 brought Willem to the throne and England into the conflict with France unambiguously on the Dutch side. The century ended, untypically, in peace but with the Dutch poised to enter what was to prove perhaps the most exhausting phase of their war effort in this period, at least as far as finance was concerned.[18]

In such a threatening environment, the underlying objective of Dutch foreign policy was not so much the pursuit of interests as the survival of the state: *raison d'état* was forced on the leaders of the Republic rather than chosen by them. The sense of being involved in a struggle for survival was strongest in the early years of the century, but continued longer than might well be thought. With the benefit of hindsight, it is easy to point to the Twelve Years Truce of 1609 with Spain as the point when the existence of the Republic as an independent state was effectively established, but for the Dutch at that time it was not quite so clear that the conflict had been decided in their favour. Whatever the logical implications of the truce, the Spanish had not formally recognised Dutch independence, and it was widely feared that, despite this agreement, they would attack again as soon it seemed to their advantage to do so. The truce in fact held, but the renewal of the war after 1621 brought a renewed sense of unease as Spanish successes – such as the taking of Breda in 1625, celebrated in the painting by Velázquez – joined with Imperial victories in the early years of the Thirty Years War. By the end of the decade, it had perhaps finally become evident that the Spanish could not defeat the Dutch but, even after the series of Swedish victories in the early 1630s, the situation in the Holy Roman Empire could still cause acute anxiety from time to time. For a brief period in the middle decades of the century this sense of a persistent threat to the survival of the Dutch state was lifted. After the Portuguese and Catalan risings of 1640, there could be little doubt about the outcome of the war with Spain and, however damaging the first two wars with England were to the Dutch economy, they were far from being a threat to the viability of the Dutch state. Such relative security, however, was short-lived, as the French attack in 1672 revived old fears, and for the rest of the century foreign policy again took on something of the nature of a struggle for survival which it had had at its beginning.

Throughout the century the chief aims of Dutch policy were essentially secular: the survival of the state, and the promotion of economic prosperity. The concept of honour which underlay the Spanish concern with 'reputación' and the French with 'gloire' was very largely foreign to Dutch statesmen. Warfare for its own sake – or rather as the proper pursuit of princes – was anathema to them, and territorial aggrandisement was never an objective. There are two possible exceptions which need to be noted at this point, however: attitudes with regard to the Spanish-ruled Netherlands, and the ambitions of successive princes of Orange. Hopes for the liberation of the whole of the Netherlands from Spain may well have lingered on into the seventeenth century, but in the event pragmatic considerations proved more powerful than any vague pan-Netherlands patriotism. The princes of Orange, on the other hand, constitute an intriguing problem: they have been accused of allowing personal and dynastic considerations too much weight in their foreign policies,[19] but a more fundamental dissonance between them and the regents of Holland in particular seems to be involved. The upbringing, education and social milieu of the princes endowed them with a set of priorities with regard to foreign policy which was perhaps rather more in tune with conventional perceptions in the rest of Europe than those of the regents. Frederik Hendrik seems to have hoped for significant territorial gains in the southern Netherlands, Willem II to have wished to resume the war against Spain in order to be able to act as a proper prince should as much as anything else, and Willem III consistently neglected the needs of the Dutch economy in order to pursue his political objectives – what might be considered a very un-Dutch way of behaving. Normally such differences were a matter of nuance and degree, but they help to remind us how unusual at the time the attitudes of the Dutch regents were.

Again, it is not a matter of arguing that the regents were proponents of a ruthless *raison d'état* – this was true of most states to a greater or lesser extent, not a distinguishing characteristic of the Dutch – but rather that the policy objectives they pursued with such single-mindedness were different. For them the interests of state were defined almost purely in economic terms: as we have seen, the Dutch saw themselves as involved in a struggle for survival for a good part of the century but, this aside, what they saw as the common interest was almost entirely the pursuit and preservation of economic success. All states at this period tried to promote economic prosperity but chiefly because this served other ends, and primarily military strength; the Dutch were different in regarding prosperity as an end in itself, and indeed as one of the prime objectives of government at every level. Such economic priorities were often obscured by the military and strategic necessities of survival in a hostile world. The long hot and cold war against France after 1672 is a case in point: for Willem III it was necessary for the preservation of the Republic, while Amsterdam and other opponents of the prince's policies were more concerned with the damage it was causing to the Dutch economy. There was also another major problem: it was not always clear that the economic interests of the individual provinces were the same. In particular, it often seemed – especially to the representatives of the other provinces – that the policies promoted by Holland were more in its own interest

than in that of the Republic as a whole. Similarly, even within Holland
there could be disagreements over economic policy between various
towns, and the common good even in economic terms was not easy to
identify. The point remains that – apart from the survival of the state
and the preservation of internal peace and order (in themselves secular
objectives) – the regents saw the pursuit of common prosperity as the
prime objective of the state, in foreign as much as in domestic policy.

The secular, particularly economic, orientation of Dutch foreign
policy is clear enough; this was indeed one of the few areas where the
provinces making up the Republic could hope to find common ground.
However, there were other, more ideological, concerns which the provinces shared, and these have tended to be somewhat neglected in
discussions of the role of the Dutch state in European politics. Despite
the pragmatic appearance of Dutch policy, it may well be that religious
considerations were more important than a superficial examination
might suggest. The Dutch regents – and the princes of Orange (but
not all their advisers) – were members of the Reformed Church and
this affected the way in which they perceived the world around them.
Admittedly, at the beginning of the century the orthodoxy of perhaps
the majority of the regents was suspect in two ways: through either
catholic or traditionalist sympathies, or leanings towards the remonstrants, a hardly less heinous crime in the eyes of the self-styled orthodox. After the crisis of 1618–19, however, the Reformed monopoly in
politics was more effectively enforced and, indeed, membership of the
same church became one quality that the regents of all seven provinces
had in common. In the perceptions of such men, protestant (especially
calvinist) powers were natural allies, while catholic states were potential
enemies; such attitudes persisted even though alliances with catholic
powers were an almost permanent necessity for the Dutch from the
moment of Henry IV of France's final conversion to catholicism in 1593
until the alliance with Austria in the last years of the seventeenth
century. An alliance with protestant England continued to be seen as
natural, even though the century was marked, after James I made
peace with Spain in 1603, by three wars and only fleeting and uncertain
agreements, before the situation was transformed by the events of
1688. It must be stressed that similar sentiments were present on the
English side also, though perhaps more strongly outside court circles
than within, especially during the reigns of Charles I and II.

This ideological view of the world with its accompanying sense of
religious duty and purpose went more or less with the grain of Dutch

policy during the long struggle with Spain, but floundered more than somewhat in the less clear-cut situation in Europe in the decades after 1648, when the peace with the Spanish seemed to have deprived the Dutch state of any very evident religious purpose. In the last decades of the century, however, the conflict with the France of Louis XIV could again be seen, at least in part, as a defence of European protestantism, and the Enterprise of England also had an unmistakable religious dimension.[20] So at both the beginning and end of the century, the question of the Republic's survival could be smoothly linked to the interests of protestantism, not only in the Republic but in Europe as a whole, to provide an ideological dimension to an otherwise pragmatic foreign policy; when these two themes diverged, however, serious doubts could arise about the nature and purpose of the Dutch state. The fierce public polemic which arose during the negotiations for the truce of 1609 are a case in point: the opponents of the truce argued not only on practical grounds that it let Spain off the hook and exposed the Republic to the danger of surprise attack whenever the Spanish felt ready, but also that *as catholics* the Spanish could not be trusted, and that the providential meaning of the Dutch state was the fight against antichrist. Without this unifying purpose the state might well fall apart, and would certainly run the risk of forfeiting god's favour. Similar arguments accompanied the approach of the final peace with Spain in 1648, but they seem to have had much less resonance in Dutch society at this time. Religiously inspired opposition to the Truce undoubtedly played a significant role in the domestic political crisis of the years after 1609; no such backlash was apparent during the crisis of 1650, when the Republic was both more prosperous and more secure than it had been in the first decades of the century. As the international atmosphere grew more threatening in the last decades of the century, and as the Dutch economy also faltered, the need for the Dutch to know that they were on god's side – and he on theirs – perhaps returned with renewed force.

The foreign policy of the Dutch state could only hope to succeed, of course, if it had the military power to back it up. Their international situation compelled the Dutch to maintain major forces on both land and sea throughout the century to ensure their survival and to protect their interests. The army was central to the struggle against Spain until 1648: whatever the opportunities and dangers of the war at sea, it was essential that the borders of the Republic be established and defended by the army on land. The land forces were reformed and reached formidable proportions in the 1590s, and continued to grow (with the interruption of the truce years) until the 1640s. After the peace with Spain, the need for a large and efficient army was much less immediately pressing; the wars with England encouraged concentration on the navy; and the army became a victim of the political wrangling over the future role of the young Willem III. The cumulative effect was a serious deterioration in its fighting quality, but the near-catastrophe of 1672 reminded the Dutch that they could not afford such neglect of the army, and under Willem's leadership it not only regained its former efficiency but became bigger than ever. The continued threat from France meant that the Republic had to remain prepared to defend itself on land for the rest of the century, and the size of the army reached new peaks in the last decade of the century and the first of the next.[21]

The navy was less central to the war effort against Spain perhaps because of the latter's relative weakness at sea, certainly in northern waters. However, the Republic needed a large and varied fleet to handle the multiplicity of tasks required of it, from blockading the Flemish coast, convoying merchant ships and protecting the herring-fishing fleet, to providing support for the army on the inland waterways.[22] Defeat in the first Anglo-Dutch war revealed the necessity for reform and in particular the creation of a battle fleet composed of ships of the line. This was achieved under the guidance of De Witt, and for the rest of the century the navy too had to be maintained at a high level of size and efficiency, because until after 1688 there was not only the challenge of the formidable French fleet, but the danger that it might combine again – as in 1672–3 – with the English navy in an attack on the Dutch. Only with the establishment of a more-or-less secure alliance with England could the Dutch afford to relax their naval vigilance.

In the light of recent analyses of the relationship between absolutism and military efficiency, it might be asked how the decentralised Dutch state was able to maintain and control such formidable armed forces. Both army and navy were Generality institutions, that is they were, formally at least, run by the central government of the Republic – indeed it did little else.[23] Although in such a decentralised polity it might have been expected that there would have been provincially organised and controlled armies, the *militie van den staet* was in fact controlled from the centre, although the system for paying it was largely provincially controlled. The navy was also formally a Generality body, but was in practice run by five admiralties which were effectively under provincial and even subprovincial control, and this showed in administrative inefficiencies and endemically poor relations between the various admiralties. Despite these weaknesses, the navy was a formidable instrument for most of the century, but they undoubtedly made it far more difficult to run efficiently. What was particularly remarkable was that the Dutch fiscal system was able to bear the strain of maintaining such large armed forces throughout the century. At a time when, for most states, prolonged involvement in war meant almost inevitable bankruptcy together with severe internal political problems, the Dutch state was able to avoid both despite having to support a large army and navy for most of the century. It was this fiscal system, and the general prosperity which supported it, which enabled the new Dutch state to play such an important part in European affairs.

The rise of the Dutch Republic to the position of a major power was astonishingly fast: in the middle of the 1580s a combination of political weakness and the formidable threat of the army of Flanders under the prince of Parma made it seem inevitable that the Dutch revolt would share the fate of most other rebellions of the early modern period, and collapse in confusion to eventual defeat; yet before the end of the century the new state had been placed on a sound footing, and by 1609 the Dutch had fought the mighty Spanish to a standstill. The Truce showed that they were a significant force in Europe, but the renewal of the war with Spain in 1621 proved them to be a major power, and for the remainder of the century they remained in the first rank of European states.

In the first half of the century – until the peace with Spain in 1648 – the Republic had a double strategic role which gave it particular significance: as the chief focus of resistance to the power of the Spanish *monarchía*, and also as the bulwark of protestantism against resurgent catholicism. The unremitting drain on resources of the long war with the Dutch played a fundamental part in sapping the power of Spain and bringing about its eclipse as a major power; the decisive moment may have been the French intervention from 1635 onwards, but the situation had been set up by the Dutch. Similarly, the Dutch attacks on their colonies and interests outside Europe were an important factor in precipitating the Portuguese revolt against Spain which was also such an important step in the definitive weakening of Spain. In the end the Spanish recognised this and elected to cut their losses by conceding in effect all Dutch demands in order to concentrate on their other problems. As a champion of protestantism, the Dutch record is less clear: they failed to rescue the Bohemian protestants and avoided direct involvement in the Thirty Years War as far as possible, leaving the dramatic role of evangelical paladin to the Swedish king, Gustavus Adolphus. Yet the continuation of the Dutch struggle with Spain, through draining Spanish resources, was a vital contribution to the eventual salvation of the protestant cause in the Holy Roman Empire. Certainly, to contemporaries the very existence of the Dutch state and its survival in the struggle with the apparently irresistible Spain was of great symbolic significance.

Yet there is a sense in which the Republic remained less eminent in this early period than its power might seem to have warranted. As a Republic, it had difficulty in finding its proper place among the powers. In terms of protocol, it had to accept a position in the international pecking order below that not just of the emperor and monarchs, but also of quite insignificant princes, and even had to cede rank to the weaker but more ancient republic of Venice.[24] Also both France and England tended to adopt a patronising attitude towards the Dutch, seeing themselves as something like (rival) sponsors of their independence. The Dutch concentrated on the war for survival and independence and had few resources and less energy to devote to anything else; it seems that only after the settlement with Spain could they lift up their heads and take a broader view of European affairs.

After 1648, the Republic entered a period of much greater mutability in international relations, but one in which its position was perhaps artificially strong because of the relative, albeit temporary, weakness of the surrounding powers, and especially France. It was indeed the resurgence of French power which brought this relatively secure period of Dutch history to an end, and ensured that after 1672 the Republic would have to concentrate on resisting the ambitions of Louis XIV. In these years the Republic's relations with England were particularly volatile, involving three wars, a short-lived alliance, and an invasion which arguably changed the course of English (and by extension British) history. The wars were indecisive, and largely limited to naval actions, but damaging to both sides; Willem III's intervention in 1688 at the very least made the change of regime in England a much smoother and less violent process than otherwise might have been the case. With regard to France, the Dutch role as animator and paymaster of a series of coalitions to hold the balance against French power, may well have been decisive in checking French expansion, but it also exposed a fundamental dilemma in Dutch policy. At a time when the Dutch economy was beginning to falter, the disruption to trade and the enormous fiscal burden of the wars with France were likely to weaken the country in the long term, but after 1672 it seemed that the threat posed by France was too great to be ignored. In the end Willem's policy was vindicated, though only after his death, by the eventual defeat of France, but the Republic was also decisively weakened by what proved indeed to be the intolerable strain of the conflict.

Although it would be going too far to suggest that the old textbook headings, which saw the predominance of Spain succeeded by that of France, be replaced by something like the century of the Dutch, nevertheless it is a salutary exercise to try to assess just how important the influence of this small, decentralised republic was in the age of the large, centralised, and absolutist monarchies. The greatest powers of the seventeenth century – Spain in its first half, France in its second – found the Dutch Republic in the way of their ambitions and could not brush it aside. The eventual defeat of these powers was not the work of the Republic alone, but the Dutch were an indispensable part of the alliances which brought about these results. Similarly, it would be an exaggeration to claim that the Dutch state saved protestantism from being overwhelmed by the power of counter-reformation catholicism and its political champions – in retrospect the protestant situation does not seem as fragile as it appeared in the somewhat paranoid vision of many contemporaries – nevertheless it was the one major power that remained unswervingly protestant – and it did act decisively to ensure that England would not be lost to the true faith.

Despite the title of this chapter, at least a brief mention of the power of the Dutch in the wider world is justified, if only because Dutch activities in both the Americas and the East were intimately connected to the conflicts within Europe: especially, of course, to the long struggle with Spain, but the wars with England were also fought to some extent outside European waters. The Dutch Republic was the first non-Iberian country to create a significant colonial empire, and its ships and men were active wherever there was profit to be made throughout the world, beginning with their first expeditions to the East in the 1590s. The activities of the VOC in India and Indonesia were, in the first decades of the century, at least an indirect contribution to the war against Spain, but commercial considerations could usually be relied upon to win out over strategic or colonial ambitions. On the other hand, the WIC was from the start much more directly intended as a means of weakening Spain by cutting at the American roots of its power, and this unrealistic objective was one of the reasons for the company's comparative failure. In the end the chief contribution which these colonial activities made to the Republic's position in Europe was the profit they made and their contribution to the country's economic pre-eminence.

Although the chief concern of Dutch traders was profit, it should not be forgotten that the circumstances outside Europe allowed or perhaps even required the use of armed force, and the Dutch soon became notorious for this, at least among those, such as the English, who were unable to compete effectively. The VOC certainly used military means to establish its position in Java and Sri Lanka, and its naval strength was a major factor in its ability to undermine Portuguese trade in the East. Similarly the English brought up the Amboina 'massacre' of 1623 at every possible opportunity, as a symbol of what were felt to be unfair Dutch practices. However, Dutch trading success in the East was in the end more the result of economic strength and trading skills than military force, though the latter helped. The Brazilian campaign highlights both the Dutch willingness to use force when it suited them and the way in which their fundamentally commercial priorities would always in the end override the colonising impulse.

The Dutch state differed from almost all others through its lack of territorial ambitions, and this orientation paradoxically marked its colonial expansion as well. The Dutch did not acquire colonial territories for their own sake but only in the service of profit: ideally they would have preferred to limit their overheads by acquiring as little land as possible. The VOC was drawn through its attempts to stabilise the political situation into controlling more and more of Java in the course of the seventeenth century, but not through any colonial intent. The attempted conquest of Brazil might seem to contradict this interpretation of Dutch aims, but in the end it reinforces them. It is true that the campaign was as much a strategic move against Spanish power in the Americas as it was an attempt to reap the profits from Brazilian sugar production, yet in the long term the failure of the Dutch state – and particularly the province of Holland – to give full support to the WIC in this area shows that trade rather than empire was the driving force behind Dutch activities in the wider world. It is the repeated attempts to conquer and control large areas of Brazil which are the exception, and which need to be explained in terms of the internal politics of the WIC and the particular problems it faced in challenging the well-entrenched Iberian power in the Americas.[25]

The Dutch did become a world power in the course of the seventeenth century, and quite quickly at that, but not in the sense or in the way that Spain had done so in the previous century. The latter's claim rested essentially on the conquest of the Aztec and Inca empires and the consequent control of large areas of central and south America; the Dutch came to control much of Java and Sri Lanka, but this territorial control was peripheral to their status as a world power. Their impact on the world outside Europe came through their trading successes; their power was economic not military or territorial. Dutch commercial interests were world-wide and perhaps only China and Australasia (for rather different reasons) were unaffected by them. In this respect they were a new phenomenon in world history.

The Dutch became a major European power in the seventeenth century, not because they wished to play a greater role in international affairs, but because they had to. They had to take part in the major conflicts of the time, not through any wish to impose their will on the rest of Europe, but because their fundamental interests and often their survival as an independent state were threatened. Ideally, perhaps, the Dutch regents would have avoided alliances and entanglements with other powers and concentrated on what they saw as their primary interests: the preservation and promotion of Dutch prosperity. Unfortunately, from this point of view, circumstances only rarely gave them the opportunity to act in this way. In the first decades of the century, the war with Spain was still a struggle for independence which the Dutch could not afford to lose, and the Thirty Years War also contained a threat to the fundamental interests and possibly the survival of the Dutch state. After 1672, France seemed to pose a similar basic threat which the Dutch could not afford to ignore, though there was, and is, room for disagreement as to how immediate this danger was. Only in the years between these two pressing challenges had the Dutch state a certain freedom of manoeuvre when it could attempt to develop a neutralist policy, and even this was disturbed by the first two Anglo-Dutch wars. Already by the end of the second war, the French invasion of the Spanish Netherlands (in the so-called War of Devolution), and the short-lived Triple Alliance to check their progress in the region, marked the end of the period when the Dutch could afford to be neutral. These circumstances meant that the Dutch state was forced to maintain a high level of expenditure on both its army and its navy throughout the century, and by the first years of the following century the strain was beginning to tell. These growing fiscal problems were partly the result of the worsening economic situation in the Republic in the later seventeenth century, but the sheer unremitting nature of the demands on Dutch finances had their own part to play. However, the decline of the Dutch Republic as a major power in the eighteenth century should perhaps not be seen simply as a consequence of these financial weaknesses. The changing nature of the major conflicts of the new century, and their physical displacement towards central Europe and away from the Dutch borders, meant that there was less immediate threat to the integrity of the Dutch state. Moreover, the rise of England, its connection with Hanover through its new dynasty, and its structural antagonism to France, made this new great power a natural ally, and indeed patron of the Dutch. In sharp contrast to the previous century, the English now saw it as one of their basic interests to prevent France from gaining control of any significant part of the Low Countries. Consequently, the Dutch could retreat to the position of a client state and relax under the protection of England.

Such a situation of peaceful obscurity, allowing the Dutch to concentrate on their economic priorities, was perhaps what they had wanted all along, and should thus be seen not as a decline but as a triumph.

2

THE ECONOMIC MIRACLE – AND ITS LIMITATIONS

The rise of the Dutch Republic to economic dominance in Europe was astonishingly rapid; its decline a slower, less obvious, though perhaps equally inexorable process. The spectacular growth of the Dutch economy helps to explain why these few provinces in the northern Netherlands could establish their independence against the might of Spain; and this success provided the financial strength that was necessary to sustain the Republic's position as a major power throughout the seventeenth century. Even the cultural triumphs of this period were, if not caused, then shaped by this prosperity and the social changes which came with it. However, if the seventeenth century witnessed the heights of Dutch success, the stagnation and economic contraction of the last decades of the century heralded the beginnings of decline. Thus the economic history of the seventeenth century is less of a story of unblemished success than used to be thought; in consequence it requires a discussion not only of the causes and nature of Dutch success but also of the later contraction, and of the possible links between the two processes.[1]

The beginnings of the Dutch economic boom can be placed tentatively in the 1590s when the worst disruptions of the struggle for independence were over – for the maritime areas, most importantly Holland, at least. The take-off was to a remarkable degree evenly spread, perhaps necessarily so, throughout all sectors of the economy. In this general process of growth, the transformation of the agricultural sector was as important as the more obvious increase in trade, or the expansion in textile manufactures. Similarly, the spectacular success of the herring fisheries should not be allowed to obscure the importance of fishing of all types, in open sea, coastal and inland. Two characteristics of this growth need to be stressed: first, that it did not come out of nothing, and secondly, that it was to a significant extent limited to Holland, especially, and the maritime provinces more generally.

The bases for the economic growth of the seventeenth century had already been laid down in the course of the previous century, if not before. Ships and traders from the northern Netherlands had already established dominance in the trade with the Baltic by the early years of the sixteenth century, the herring fisheries had possibly already reached their peak before the Revolt, and the structural transformation of the rural sector was well on the way before the 'Golden Century' began to glisten. These developments did not make the later successes inevitable nor, indeed, can they fully explain them, but it is clear that without this period of preparation the boom could not have taken place at all, never mind as rapidly as it did.

However, the economic transformation of the seventeenth century was very largely confined to Holland and, to a somewhat lesser extent, the other maritime regions. The land provinces – Gelderland, Overijssel, Utrecht, States Brabant – were not unaffected by the momentous changes which were taking place in Holland, but they were largely excluded from this new prosperity and the structural transformation that accompanied it. There were at least two economies in the Republic in the seventeenth century, and only one of them was the epitome of commercial capitalism[2] that is associated with the Dutch situation at this time.

The demographic history of the region in the sixteenth and seventeenth centuries reflects these regional differences. The population of the northern Netherlands as a whole grew from around or just under a million at the beginning of the sixteenth century to about 1 500 000 at the start of the seventeenth century, and continued growing till it reached a peak of something under 2 000 000 in its last decades. So the total population more or less doubled in these centuries, but a large part of this growth came from one province alone. The population of Holland rose from c.275 000 in 1514 to c.672 000 in 1622 and peaked around 1680 at an estimated 883 000.[3] Zeeland and Friesland followed the Holland pattern rather more weakly, while the land provinces produced a much flatter demographic curve.

The period of Dutch economic dominance was relatively short-lived: it did not cover the whole of the century, but was already faltering by its third quarter, and evidence is beginning to accumulate which would place the definitive turning point at around 1670. Certainly, there were significant signs of overall decline by the end of the century. In most of Holland, population growth had already ceased by the middle of the century, and even the largest towns – Amsterdam, Leiden, Rotterdam, Haarlem, The Hague – had reached their peak by about the 1670s, and subsequently stagnated or even declined. By this time agricultural prices and rents had similarly hit the buffers after over a century of steady growth, interrupted only by the first years of the Revolt. Manufactures were also beginning to lose foreign markets through high costs at home and mercantilist policies abroad. The picture is not one of unremitting gloom: trade and shipping held out rather longer, and it may well be that definitive decline in this area can be put as late as the 1740s,[4] while some industries such as the Delft potteries continued to flourish into the eighteenth century, and Gouda actually grew in population – on the basis of its pipe-making industry – at a time when most of the manufacturing towns were already in serious trouble. Notoriously too, growing economic problems did not halt the expansion of gin- and brandy-distilling. However, there can be little doubt that by the last third of the century the years of general expansion and success were over, and the Dutch had entered a new and much more problematic period in their economic history.

Throughout this period the land provinces had a markedly different economic history. The population of these regions grew much more slowly and uncertainly, particularly in comparison to the population explosion of the maritime provinces, and there was little if any increase in the degree of urbanisation. However, their economies were transformed in the long term by the powerful influence of the boom in the maritime areas, and especially by the pull of the Holland market.[5] Their trading towns in particular suffered from the competition of the more dynamic towns of Holland, and the same could be said for many of their manufactures, though the expanding market provided by the growth in the maritime region proved a stimulus to others, such as paper-making in the Veluwe. Also before the end of the seventeenth century, low rural wages together with the fundamental problems of the Holland textile industry were beginning to pull wool and linen textile manufacture into the Twente region of Overijssel and North Brabant.

Indeed, just as the great boom of the Dutch economy had been largely restricted to the maritime regions, so the worst effects of the decline were felt there also, and the land provinces, though not experiencing a wholly favourable time proved considerably more buoyant economically. Indeed, it might be said that the economic decline of the eighteenth century was the beginning of a process which would eventually bring the two disparate regions of the Republic much closer together in wealth and social development. This reduction of the economic and social differences between the two groups of provinces may have made possible the unitary state of the nineteenth century.

The economic success of the seventeenth century was built on foundations already laid before the Revolt, and in particular the rapidity of Dutch expansion from the 1590s onwards cannot be understood without taking this background into consideration. Although the northern regions of the Netherlands, even Holland and Zeeland, were overshadowed by the more spectacular trading and manufacturing successes of the great towns of Flanders and Brabant in the fifteenth and early sixteenth centuries, fundamental – even structural – changes were taking place which prepared the way for later developments. Again, it must be stressed that the changes were restricted to the maritime provinces and, indeed, in a great measure to Holland alone.

In the first place, there was a remarkably high level of urbanisation: the towns of Holland were nothing like as large as the greater towns of the southern Netherlands, but there were many of them, and already by the middle of the sixteenth century about half the population of the province lived in towns. This was in sharp contrast to the general situation in Europe, and even considerably outstripped the degree of urbanisation of Flanders and Brabant; even before the economic expansion of the early seventeenth century, Holland was fundamentally different from the rest of Europe. Another area which was a pointer to the future was the increasing domination of ships and merchants from the northern Netherlands in the trade between the Baltic and the rest of Europe. This trade – principally in grain from north-eastern Europe and later to be referred to as the *moeder negocie* or mother trade – produced significant profits, employed large numbers of ships and men, and also provided the reliable supply of cheap bread grains which allowed Holland's agriculture to move away from arable to dairying and other more profitable branches of farming. It also encouraged the development of shipbuilding and a group of other manufactures – such as sailmaking and sawmilling – associated with the construction and fitting-out of ships. This sector was also stimulated by the demand for ships and services coming from the fishing industry. The fish of the innumerable lakes and rivers of the maritime region were a very important resource, especially before the large-scale drainages of the early seventeenth century, and the Zuyder Zee, the estuary of the Maas, and the coastal waters in general were also important fishing grounds, but the North Sea herring fishery was perhaps most important in that it provided a high-quality export product, as well as employment for large numbers of men and specialised fishing boats. The introduction of a technique for preserving the herring while still at sea allowed for longer periods at the fishing grounds, encouraged the use of larger boats, and opened the way for major expansion. In fact it seems that the herring fishery may have reached a peak in terms of catch and men employed by the middle years of the sixteenth century; during the early Republic it may have become better organised and more efficient in some ways, but not bigger.[6]

The towns of Holland were already pursuing a wide range of manufacturing activities in the early sixteenth century, but there were many problems in this area and few, if any, unequivocal successes. The textile industry was present in most, and important in some towns, but was in decline overall because of changes in the market and competition from new types of cloth produced by innovatory techniques in the southern Netherlands. Only after the Revolt, and partly as a result of southern immigration, would this sector solve its structural problems and enter a boom period. Brewing had been very important in Holland in the fifteenth century not only for supplying the home market but for its exports as well, particularly to the south, but for a variety of reasons it could not sustain this position, and it became clear in the course of the following century that the industry was in full decline, with serious effects on the economies of towns such as Gouda and Haarlem. This, in fact, was one area of production that would never regain its former greatness, especially not in terms of exports. However, if the problems of such traditional industries as these caused major economic difficulties for many of the Holland towns, compensation was beginning to be provided by activities linked with the expansion of shipping and fishing. The demand for ships and boats of all kinds was high and rising in the sixteenth century, especially when the importance of boats and barges for transport within the northern Netherlands is taken into account. Shipbuilding in its turn stimulated sawmilling, rope- and sailmaking and similar activities, while the herring fisheries began to turn barrel-making into an important industry. Such developments also gave a further boost to trade, as the wood needed for shipbuilding had to be imported – largely from Norway – while the preservation of herring demanded high-quality salt which had to be brought from France and Portugal.

Perhaps most important of all, however, was the crisis in the rural sector and the way it began to be resolved. By the late fifteenth century, an apparent rise in sea level combined with the constant shrinkage of drained land was making water control more and more difficult and creating problems especially for arable farming. The problem was exacerbated by the long-term effects of peat-digging – about the only fuel available in the region for domestic or industrial use. The consequent difficulties were perhaps most acute in the Northern Quarter of Holland, but they were also significant for the province as a whole. In the long term this problem was tackled if not solved by the vast reclamation projects of the late sixteenth and early seventeenth centuries, but before this took place the Holland farmers found themselves forced to switch from the cultivation of bread grains to crops such as oats and barley which were more suitable to the conditions, and to cattle for dairy-farming or beef production.[7] This process involved both an increasing involvement in the market and an ever greater integration into the economy of the towns. In the first place, it was the availability of relatively cheap grain from the Baltic which made the shift away from arable both possible and economically attractive. Also the growing towns not only provided a market for the farmers but also proved capable of absorbing the surplus rural population generated by the switch to less labour-intensive types of farming. Fishing, seafaring and rural manufactures also provided income and employment and helped to diversify the rural economy, especially in North Holland. The development of an increasingly efficient, varied and especially market-oriented rural sector was an essential prerequisite for the modernisation of the region's economy as a whole. These developments in agriculture spread throughout the maritime provinces, but not to the land provinces where the pressures operating on the rural economy were very different.[8]

To put it briefly, the maritime region of the northern Netherlands, and especially the province of Holland, was by about the middle of the sixteenth century already marked by economic and social characteristics which made it very different from the rest of Europe. In degree of urbanisation and the transformation of the rural sector it was more advanced than the apparently more successful economies of Flanders and Brabant, and the growth in its shipping and fisheries was also a sign of considerable economic resilience. These preconditions did not make the spectacular successes of the following century inevitable, but they certainly made them possible.

When contemporaries looked with envy at the prosperity of the Dutch Republic in the seventeenth century certain things stood out while others, perhaps of equal importance or almost so, were disregarded or not even noticed. They saw – and even exaggerated – the vast numbers of Dutch merchant ships operating in the waters all around Europe; they were aware of the efficiency of the textile industry of Leiden and Haarlem; they were impressed by the Amsterdam Bourse and the Exchange Bank; and competitors, certainly, were impressed by the efficient way the Dutch dominated the herring fisheries. Although the evident prosperity of the countryside, particularly in the west, was occasionally remarked upon, there was surprisingly little comment on the innovatory techniques and the far-reaching orientation to the market which was transforming the rural sector. Such commentaries are interesting, especially in so far as they reveal the ways in which Dutch society differed from the norms which these visitors brought with them, but they do not necessarily tell us what it was that made the Dutch economy the success it was or, indeed, just what the nature of that success was.

The outstanding feature of the Dutch economy, and what made it perhaps the first capitalist economy, was the thorough penetration of the market and the high degree of integration brought about by market forces. One way of understanding this development is to see it as the economy which had been characteristic of the trading towns of the region now being expanded to domination of the country as a whole. Another way of beginning to understand what was going on is to see Holland – which was the essential locus of this structural transformation – as if it were a single town, with the numerous towns of the province combining into an urban system, as a sort of forerunner of the modern *randstad*.[9] Whether seen as the pioneer of the modern economy, or as the acme of the late medieval urban economy – and there is something to be learnt from both approaches to an understanding of the Dutch seventeenth century – this domination by the market sets the Republic off sharply from the rest of contemporary Europe, where the inroads of the capitalist system had made relatively little impact on the economy as a whole. In this respect, at least, the land provinces of the Republic had possibly more in common with Holland than they had with the rest of Europe. Their responses to market pressures may have been different from those of the maritime region, but they were hardly less influenced by such forces than Holland itself. The Dutch economy might well have stood, and possibly did stand, as a model for the capitalist system of Adam Smith's *Wealth of Nations*.[10]

Fundamental to this new sort of economy, of course, was a not only an intense trading system within the country but also the extension of Dutch commercial power and influence throughout much of Europe and, eventually, a good part of the extra-European world as well. As has been seen, Dutch trade in Europe was already well developed before the Revolt, and particularly in what have come to be referred to as the bulk trades. Merchants and ships from the northern Netherlands were already moving towards control of the trade in Baltic grain by the early sixteenth century, and commerce through the Sound became one of the foundations of overall Dutch success in the following century. Already by this time almost 70 per cent of the ships passing through the Sound and paying toll were Dutch and, even taking account of those not paying the toll, the Dutch share of this trade remained around 50 per cent throughout the first half of the century. After some disruption in the early decades of the Revolt, Dutch domination of the Baltic trade measured by both number of ships and tonnage carried became even more marked.[11] There has been some disagreement over the role of this trade in the rise of the Dutch economy[12] but, while the bulk trades in themselves could not constitute trading primacy, this could not have been achieved without them. Besides being one of the main pillars of Dutch commercial success, the grain trade was also exemplary of the nature of their trading hegemony. In the first instance, the import of bread grains, chiefly rye, from Danzig and other Baltic ports was to supply the needs of the market in the Netherlands, a demand which accelerated as the agriculture of lower-lying regions moved away from arable. However, the general population rise of the sixteenth century created a need for grain in other parts of Europe as well, and the Dutch grip on Baltic grain allowed them to move in to service this expanding market in France, Spain, and then the Mediterranean. Dutch factors would buy up grain, ship it to Amsterdam and store it there in warehouses, then sell it on when the demand – and thus the price – was highest elsewhere. The operation of a staple market of this sort was a basic characteristic of Dutch trading success; merchants, particularly from Holland, used their trading skills and contacts, together with their superior financial resources, to buy up goods in one part of Europe, store it in their home towns, and then sell it on to other parts of the continent when and where a profit could be made.[13] One of the advantages the Dutch had over their rivals was that they could afford to buy early and wait longer for a profitable market. Rotterdam specialised in the trade in French wines and, working through their agents in Nantes and Bordeaux, its merchants would buy up the grape harvest well in advance, gaining relatively cheap prices in return for the risks they were taking. So Holland, and particularly Amsterdam, acted not just as a warehouse but as a middleman for Europe for a whole range of goods. The advantages that the Dutch gained from this function came not just in the form of profits from trade and of opportunities for a whole range of traders and brokers, but also through the large-scale employment which the system directly created for seamen, lightermen, dockers and warehouse-workers. This flow of goods through the Republic also provided opportunities for the development of industries to process raw materials and semi-finished products, thus adding further value – and profit – to the trade and providing more employment.

The flow of products organised by the staple market was largely carried in Dutch ships, and the growth of the Dutch merchant fleet was intimately connected to the development of this system. Shipping was a most visible area of Dutch success: Dutch ships could be seen everywhere and in such numbers as to cause contemporaries to exaggerate their total wildly.[14] The merchant fleet had in fact grown to something like 2000 seagoing ships, excluding the herring *buizen*, by the middle of the seventeenth century.[15] The bulk trades in grain, wood and other naval stores with the Baltic and Scandinavia had encouraged the design and use of new, specialised cargo ships, in particular the *fluit* (flute), which had better cargo-carrying qualities and could be sailed by smaller crews than their competitors. This efficiency of operation had the drawback of making the ships less easy to defend, but on the whole this was not too great a problem in northern waters, though the losses to the Dunkirk privateers and in the wars with England are a reminder of the vulnerability of these new, specialised cargo ships.[16]

Another pillar of the sixteenth-century economy which continued to be of vital importance during the boom years was fishing, particularly for herring. In a country with few useful raw materials, North Sea herring acted as a home-grown product even though much of it was caught off the English and Scottish coasts – much to the irritation of the Scots and English – and provided a valuable article for export, especially to the Baltic and to Cologne for redistribution in Germany, where catholic regions provided a particularly grateful market. Dutch success was based on the specialised fishing-boat (*buis*) and technical innovations, particularly in curing the catch at sea which produced a higher quality product and allowed the fleet to stay on the fishing grounds longer. In the seventeenth century this fishery may not have grown much if at all over the previous century's peak, but perhaps it became more organised with greater integration between fishing, curing and barrelling, and the export trade. Both the merchant and the fishing fleet provided employment for thousands of seamen directly, and indirectly for workers in a number of shore-based activities serving the needs of these ships, from cooperage to the baking of ships' biscuits. Moreover, the demand for large numbers of ships and boats was the bedrock on which a successful shipbuilding industry was built, and this in turn stimulated the timber trade which was carried on by specialised Dutch ships. This interconnection of various sectors in the Dutch economy was one of its great strengths in the years of growth, as expansion in one area created demand in others, but it also become a source of vulnerability later, as problems in one area turned out to have serious knock-on effects in others. The growth of Dutch manufactures in the seventeenth century, thus, was in part dependent on the success of the trading economy in bringing raw materials and semi-finished goods into the country, and in finding markets abroad. The most successful Dutch industries were dependent on processing imported materials and needed to export much of their produce to survive. The textile industries of Leiden and Haarlem relied on imported wool, linen, and in some cases semi-finished cloth, and exported a significant proportion of their production; their catastrophic decline in the late seventeenth and eighteenth centuries was a consequence of falling price-competitiveness and tariff barriers which inexorably deprived them of their foreign markets. Shipbuilding was somewhat different as it initially expanded to serve the needs of the growing merchant marine and fishing fleet; although the peak it achieved by the late seventeenth century was partly dependent on foreign sales, as long as the home demand for ships and boats of a wide range of types remained high the industry could thrive. However, it did depend on imported raw materials, in this case wood imported from Scandinavia, particularly Norway, with Hoorn as the centre of the trade. The success of the industry was also linked to technological innovation in the design of wind-powered sawmills and methods of prefabrication, for example. Among the reasons shipbuilding became concentrated in the region of the Zaan were good communication by water for the supply of timber and the delivery of the finished ships, and the availability of ample space for innumerable windmills to exploit the prevailing winds.

New techniques were also important in the textile industry, although here they were to a significant extent imported from the southern Netherlands. There was some textile production in most of the towns of Holland, but it had become increasingly centred on Leiden and Haarlem in the course of the sixteenth century. Even – or especially – here the industry seemed in terminal decline until it was boosted by the influx of refugees and other immigrants from the textile centres of the south from the 1580s onwards. These newcomers brought with them the techniques for making the light mixed-fibre cloths – says, bays, fustians – which were the core of the new draperies in the South. The immigrants also brought new organisational techniques, considerable capital resources, and extensive commercial contacts, all of which helped to make the textile industry one of the great successes of the early seventeenth century. In general, the Dutch lacked natural advantages over their rivals: they did not have privileged access to important raw materials, and wage levels were relatively high. In consequence, advantages in technique to give an edge either in price or in quality were essential if Dutch manufacturers were to dominate their home market, let alone export successfully. A good example of this process are the *trafieken*, a term denoting branches of industry refining or processing imported materials, often from outside Europe, such as sugar-refining and tobacco-processing. There was a whole range of such manufactures, and they were peculiarly sensitive to changing market conditions, as the Dutch had no built-in advantages over potential rivals either in the procuring of the raw materials or in the sale of the finished articles elsewhere in Europe. Apart from technological change in the narrow sense, the Dutch manufacturing sector could exploit considerable infrastructural advantages. Not only was it served by an efficient trading and shipping sector which was extremely adept at supplying raw materials cheaply and finding suitable markets for manufactures, but also the transport system within the country facilitated easy and relatively cheap movement of goods by water along a dense network of canals and rivers. Although the *Zaanstreek* was almost in the middle of Holland, there was no problem in supplying the region with timber by water from Hoorn, and there was easy access for the ships it built along the river Zaan itself to the Zuider Zee. The economic importance of the inland waterways meant that the towns fought fiercely, particularly during the period of the great drainage projects, to protect their interests in this regard. The political power and autonomy of the Holland towns often meant that changes which might have improved the communications of the province as a whole were blocked by towns who feared that they would be disadvantaged.[17]

This intense conflict between the towns of Holland over water communications was partly caused by the extent of the drainage undertaken in the early seventeenth century. In this period the Northern Quarter of Holland was turned into a solid landmass for the first time by the drainage of the Beemster, Schermer and other big inland lakes.[18] It has been calculated that agricultural land in Holland increased by more than a third in the course of the early modern period, and that of this total at least half was produced in the 60 years from the 1590s onwards. The proportional gain in Zeeland was probably even greater and agricultural land increased by close to a third in the alluvial region as a whole.[19] Although some land was reclaimed from the sea, most of the new land came from inland drainage. The need for radical measures had become acute by the early sixteenth century, with the combination of apparently rising sea levels and the sinking of the land in long-established polders causing ever greater problems in water control, and the economic upturn after the Revolt was a stimulus to action. These drainage schemes were made possible by the improved pumping power of the new windmills, which allowed greater depths of water to be pumped out and kept dry, but the incentive came from rising agricultural prices and rents, which in turn were a consequence of the transformation and growing prosperity of the rural sector, at least in the maritime regions of the country. Most of the necessary finance seems to have come from investors in the towns of Holland, for whom the drainage schemes seemed to offer a profitable, but above all secure, place for their spare capital in an economy where safe investments were rather hard to find.

Although the effects of the drainage and reclamation projects were most spectacular in the Northern Quarter of Holland, significant results were also achieved in Holland south of the IJ, Zeeland, Friesland and Groningen, and it was only in this period – most of these projects were carried out in the first half of the seventeenth century – that the countryside of these maritime provinces began to take on the

meticulously manicured appearance it presents today. Before this
phase there were far more lakes, ponds, marshes, rivers and streams,
and in many areas travel was easier by water than by land, but if the
amount of water and the difficulty of controlling it caused major problems for agriculture, there had also been considerable compensations.
In particular the drainage process was a major blow to river and lake
fishing, which had up to that point been an important source of food
and profit for the rural population.[20] Also some towns and many
villages found that their communications with the sea were becoming
considerably less convenient. The transformation of Holland's countryside not only opened up opportunities for many, it also closed down
others.

For, if the physical changes to the land were the most immediately
obvious, these were a consequence of the more profound transformation of economic and social relationships in the countryside of Holland
and the other western provinces which took place during the sixteenth
and seventeenth centuries. Put simply, agriculture began to concentrate
on production for the market, and to specialise in those areas for which
the low-lying land was best fitted. In turn this meant that farming had
to shed its surplus labour, and earn enough money to buy those goods
it was no longer producing for itself, as well as to pay for services
farmers no longer had time to perform for themselves. Specifically,
there was a general shift away from arable, especially grain, farming
in favour of pastoral activities. Dairy-farming and the fattening-up of
beef calves – many of them imported from as far away as Denmark –
were probably most important in Holland, although there was also an
intensification of market-gardening to serve the needs of the growing
towns, and in the course of the century specialised arable activities also
emerged such as the cultivation of tulips, which survived the collapse of
the notorious craze of the 1630s.

The tight integration of the Dutch economy is again significant here,
for this concentration on producing for the market, initially that provided by the towns of Holland, but in the long term for export as well,
was only possible because cheap imports were available to meet the
needs that Dutch agriculture no longer found it profitable to supply. In
this respect the availability of cheap grain from the Baltic, and the
control exercised by Dutch merchants on this trade, was an important
prerequisite for the increasing efficiency of Dutch agriculture. Also the
economic buoyancy of the towns of Holland in the early seventeenth
century not only created a growing demand and rising prices for the

products of local agriculture, but also proved able to absorb the surplus rural population created by the shift to less labour-intensive activities. The thorough economic integration of town and countryside in Holland – and to a somewhat lesser extent in the other maritime provinces – was a mark of the relative modernity of its economy as a whole. However, this intimate connection between all sectors meant that problems in one had effects throughout the system: whether the declining agricultural prices and rents of the last third of the century were a cause or a consequence of the overall downturn of the economy is perhaps the wrong question to ask; they are better seen as one part – important but nevertheless only a part – of a complex interaction which brought to an end the not-so-long boom of the Dutch economy well before the last years of the Golden Century.

At every stage of its development, and certainly at its peak, the Dutch economy was heavily dependent on profitable economic relations with the rest of Europe. Trade with other countries was an indispensable characteristic of the economic system, which was the very polar opposite of an autarchy. The most successful of Dutch manufactures could not be sustained on domestic demand alone and required foreign markets; the prosperity, too, of the fisheries depended on being able to export a significant proportion of their catch. Agricultural exports, similarly, were an important aspect of the economy of many rural areas in the developed west and north of the country. Amsterdam became an important financial market, and Dutch finance reached far beyond the borders of the Republic before the end of the century;[21] and, of course, commerce and shipping provided services for the European economy that others could either not provide or not as efficiently. In consequence, to look just at the nature of the growing Dutch economy is only part of an explanation of its success; it is also necessary to examine the context in which the Dutch were operating.

The temptation is to label the Dutch as a parasitic economy, which flourished only because of the weaknesses of others. This was certainly one of the common reactions at the time: it became a cliché of contemporary economic thought – if that is the right term for a rather less than rigorous form of discourse – to blame the Dutch for any problems in one's own economy. The English in particular saw the Dutch as flourishing at their expense: making a fortune out of catching English fish, exploiting English weaknesses by monopolising the finishing of English cloth – thought to be the most profitable phase of manufacture

– and in general blocking English commercial progress not only in Europe but, perhaps even more gallingly, in extra-European trade as well.[22] The French too saw the Dutch as a major obstruction to French economic growth – such was, notoriously, the view of Louis XIV's finance minister, Colbert. However, such opinions rested on conceptions about the nature of the international economy which were of dubious validity even at the time they were written. Contemporaries considered trade, and prosperity in general, to be a more or less fixed commodity, such that if one country became richer then others must inevitably become poorer. Such primitive conceptions of the nature of the international economy and the consequences of competition are certainly not true of the modern world economy – *pace* the rhetoric of politicians and economists who should know better – but it may be doubted whether they held much water in the seventeenth century either.

However, it may well be that the Dutch economy was able to boom not because it was parasitic on the rest of Europe, but because it was able to provide services that other countries could not provide for themselves, at least with any efficiency, at the time. The standard view is still that the seventeenth century was a period of stagnation or depression for the European economy as a whole.[23] Even those who argue that there were too many exceptions to this rule for the idea of a general depression to be acceptable are forced to agree that large parts of Europe – including France, the Holy Roman Empire, Italy and Spain, which is in all conscience a good part of the continent – did experience severe economic difficulties in this period.[24] The Dutch economy flourished in this apparently hostile atmosphere partly because it could supply services which a more developed European economy might not have needed.

To the extent that the Dutch trading economy depended on its staple market function, it could be said to rely on the European economy as a whole being too little developed to be able to do without a middleman. By the same token it can be argued that when the European commercial and financial system began to develop again, it would in time be able to dispense with the services of an intermediary economy – which is what seems to have happened in the course of the eighteenth century. Meanwhile the poor articulation of the European economy meant that if a seller of rye in Danzig needed to find a buyer in Livorno, then both made use of the Dutch market. This gave employment to Dutch factors, ships and seamen, lightermen and dockers, and brought profits to Dutch merchants and shipowners, but this was hardly a parasitic process, and most complaints came from those who wanted to carry out the same function but were less efficient than the Dutch. So the Dutch economy provided an entrepôt service which Europe needed during the century or so of economic difficulties following the sixteenth-century boom, but it would last only as long as it was convenient to the merchants of the rest of Europe: when foreign traders found it possible and profitable to by-pass the Dutch market then they would do so, and the Dutch would not be able to prevent it.

Dutch manufacturers were only able to expand to the extent they did during the seventeenth century because they were able to capture foreign markets for their products, and this could certainly be seen by contemporaries as a form of exploitation. Given the chance, the Dutch could certainly be ruthless in the suppression of competition when it suited them. When, in accordance with the propositions of alderman Cockayne, the English government in 1614 banned the export of white (or semi-finished) cloths in the hope of stimulating the growth of a domestic cloth-finishing industry, the Republic promptly banned the import of finished cloth from England and the project collapsed. It was not just that the English could not build-up a finishing sector from scratch, at least not quickly enough, but that they would not have been able to find markets for the cloths even if they had. For over a century, the Merchant Adventurers had been relying on a staple for the distribution of their cloths on the continent of Europe; they did not themselves have the network of traders to bring the goods to the buyers. By the seventeenth century the northern Netherlands had taken over this function from Antwerp; it was only slowly that the English economy was able to emancipate itself from what seemed to some the thrall of Dutch dominance in such areas. However, the ability of the Dutch to impose their will in this way was strictly limited in Europe – colonial trade was another matter – and the successes of Leiden and Haarlem textiles, *Zaanstreek* shipbuilding, Delft pottery, Gouda pipe-making and so on were due to lower prices, higher quality or both. Effective use of old techniques and economies of scale as well as technological innovation helped to give Dutch manufacturers the edge, but this was a fragile and vulnerable advantage. Mercantilist theory recommended the development of domestic industry and its protection by various means, including subsidies and tariff barriers. When the surrounding countries began to adopt such measures – beginning with Colbert's punitive tariffs of 1667 – there was little or nothing the Dutch could do, particularly as theirs was a relatively high-wage economy. The rhythmn of decline varied from industry to industry, but the process itself was ineluctable.

The long-distance trade flows were not only managed to a great extent by Dutch merchants, the goods were carried by Dutch ships, and the apparent ubiquity of Dutch shipping was a more visible aspect of Dutch economic strength during this century than the much less evident financial presence. Ships from the northern Netherlands were already beginning to dominate the Baltic trade by the middle of the sixteenth century, Dutch ships handled much of the carrying trade of the North Sea region by the early decades of the seventeenth, and by the middle of that century they had penetrated the Mediterranean – being held up only by the continued war with Spain up to this point. Quite how profitable the carrying trade alone was is a matter of controversy among modern specialists, but it cannot be denied that the sheer size of the merchant fleet made it a vital source of employment in the maritime provinces, and the need for ships formed the basis of the prosperity of the shipyards of Zaandam and elsewhere.

One of the reasons which have been given for the seventeenth-century depression in Europe is the high incidence of warfare, disrupting trade, finance and shipping. What is remarkable about the Dutch experience was their ability to thrive despite their almost constant involvement in war. As we have seen, the war with Spain continued with only a short intermission up till 1648 and the series of wars with France began in 1672, and even the relatively peaceful intervening period was interrupted by two wars with England which were particularly damaging to Dutch shipping. It is not that the Dutch economy was unaffected by the wars, but that it might well have done even better without them[25] – the Dutch certainly thought so. Their breakthrough in the Spanish trade, for example, could only come after the ending of hostilities between the two countries, but in a very few years after 1648 Dutch traders swept to dominance in this trade, brushing aside their English rivals in the process and providing one stimulus to the First Anglo-Dutch War.[26] Similarly, the Thirty Years War caused problems in Dutch trade with the Baltic, particularly in the 1620s. In fact, far from being able to play the role of an economic *tertium gaudens* benefiting from the misfortunes of others, the Dutch themselves were as heavily involved in war as any other country in Europe. Admittedly, after the 1580s the key maritime region was almost completely free of direct disruption by warfare in the form of invasion or pillage, but on the other hand the Dutch economy was more heavily reliant on trade than any other, and its seaborne trade in particular was vulnerable to acts of war. Dutch merchant ships, unless specially prepared for dangerous areas, were practically unarmed and, along with the fishing fleet, provided an attractive target for enemy warships and privateers. The Dutch ideal was peaceful trade in a peaceful Europe, but they were rarely able even to approximate this condition.

The Dutch economy also acted as a magnet for immigrants: there were religious and political motives for such immigration, but undoubtedly the chief reason was economic. During its century of prosperity the Dutch economy was short of workers, not of employment, and it drew in seasonal, temporary and permanent immigrants from the area around the North Sea and north-western Europe in particular.[27] The first great wave of migration came from the southern provinces of the Netherlands from the 1580s onwards, a movement whose influence on the development of the North was – literally – incalculable.[28] Many of these were, of course, religious refugees fleeing before the reimposition of Spanish rule and intolerant catholicism in the South, but the element of economic motivation should not be ignored. The disruption to the economy of the southern provinces caused by the continuation of the war, and also by the blockade of the mouth of the Schelde by the Dutch, brought both merchants and artisans to the North in search of better conditions, and their presence was a significant stimulus to the textile industries of Leiden and Haarlem, and to the international commercial contacts of Amsterdam. Later the Republic, and Holland in particular, attracted large numbers of men and women[29] from north-west Germany and Scandinavia who took employment in a large range of capacities, notably as seamen and maidservants. The population of Amsterdam could not have grown at the rate it did without large-scale immigration,[30] and both the fishing and the merchant fleets employed considerable numbers of foreign seamen. The Dutch economy offered opportunities which were lacking in the surrounding areas, and many who had intended to return home in fact settled permanently in the Republic.

One final aspect of the Dutch economic impact on Europe which needs at least to be touched on is the financial strength of the Dutch. This expressed itself in a number of ways, but most obviously in the ubiquity of Dutch capital throughout much of northern and western Europe, and the availability of relatively cheap money at home. Dutch capital could be found draining French marshes, developing the

Swedish copper and iron industry, and exploiting the monopoly of Austrian quicksilver, and Amsterdam became the financial centre of Europe before the end of the century. One of the reasons for this success was that money could be obtained more cheaply and easily here than elsewhere in Europe; interest rates remained surprisingly low as for much of the century capital was chasing safe investments. The speed with which the starting capital of the VOC and West India Company was subscribed in the first decades of the century is symptomatic both of the amount of domestic capital available and of the eagerness of Dutch investors to take part in promising ventures. Similarly the ease with which the province of Holland could raise loans despite the low rates of interest it was willing to pay suggests that the demand for secure investments overshot the supply. All branches of the economy benefited from the possibility of borrowing money cheaply, and this facility was a particular boon to merchants working in the staple market.

To contemporaries perhaps the most impressive aspect of Dutch economic success in the Golden Century was the establishment of the first major extra-European empire by a non-Iberian power. Only Spain and Portugal had succeeded in establishing significant colonies in the sixteenth century, and the achievements of France and even England were minimal before the eighteenth century, but meanwhile the Dutch were able to establish a trading empire such as the world had never before seen.[31] For a brief period the Dutch were not just the major economic power in Europe but did indeed seem to approach 'primacy in world trade'.[32]

Dutch overseas expansion was different in type from the Spanish or even the Portuguese in that it was primarily concerned with trade, with bringing colonial products to Europe and selling them at a profit. All else was secondary and, indeed, the foundation of true colonies was avoided as far as possible as they were regarded as a potential drag on trade. Although by the early eighteenth century the Dutch controlled Java and much of Sri Lanka, these conquests had been undertaken with reluctance, and the expense of taking and holding these regions may have significantly weakened the finances of the VOC in the long run. The Dutch in the main did not want to found colonies but to make a profit; the strength of the VOC was that it kept this priority firmly in mind, the weakness of the WIC that it failed to do so. Even where colonies – of a sort – were established in New Netherland and the Cape of Good Hope, the ambivalent attitudes of the respective companies meant that neither was a real success: the WIC could not decide what to do with the former, and the VOC wanted the Cape merely as a place where its ships could take on fresh food and water, and had no interest in its development beyond this function. The attempt to wrest Brazil from the Portuguese is an exception which at least in part proves the rule. Brazil became a target in the 1620s and '30s because it was the most vulnerable of the economically attractive areas of Spanish-controlled America; after initial success the Dutch failed to hold on essentially because Holland lost interest – with the Portuguese revolt against Spain and then the end of the Eighty Years War, the conquest of Brazil lost its strategic purpose, and Dutch merchants could hope to make profits out of the Brazilian sugar trade without the expense of conquering and controlling the region. By the late 1640s normal Dutch priorities had reasserted themselves and the Brazilian adventure was doomed.

The Dutch trading 'empire' differed also in the sheer extent of its geographical range. To some extent this was anticipated by the Portuguese system of trading posts in the East, but the Dutch had more factories, more ships, more traders and more money. In the course of less than a century they established a trading system which included in the Americas, as well as New Netherland, Curaçao and other islands in the Caribbean, and Surinam (even after their retreat from Brazil), and a major position in the trade supplying slaves to the Spanish and Portuguese colonies.[33] The necessary slaves were supplied by their posts on the East African coast, and the VOC had established control of the Cape of Good Hope. The greatest success was in the East where they were active on both coasts of India, came to dominate the trade of Sri Lanka, controlled Java and the Moluccas (the spice islands), had a strong position in Malaysia, controlled Taiwan for a while, and from 1639 were the sole European power allowed to trade with Japan. (They also explored the western coast of Australia, but abandoned it as useless as far as commerce was concerned.) Dutch commercial experience and expertise enabled them to out-trade their competitors, particularly the Portuguese, and this was particularly important in trade in Asia itself. The central problem for all European traders to the East was that they needed gold and silver coin to buy Eastern goods, as there was little or no market for European products in Asia. The VOC tried to cut down on bullion outflows by building up an extensive network of inter-Asian trade in the hope of making enough profit to pay for the commodities it was sending to Europe. This attempt was, however, never entirely successful.

Dutch ships began to appear in Eastern waters in the 1590s, and in 1602 the VOC was founded to coordinate Dutch efforts in the region. The primary aim in its early years was the control of the spice trade with Europe, and the main target was the Portuguese trading network. The company had astonishing success: within half a century a combination of force and trading skills had made them the chief supplier of spices to Europe and they had a monopoly of Moluccan cloves, though pepper – the most important item in the trade – was too widely produced to be controlled to the extent the Dutch had hoped. From their base in Batavia (present-day Djakarta) the governors-general of the company controlled an enormously wide and complex system of trade, and the shipments of oriental goods to Europe brought large profits to the VOC and a significant access of prosperity to the Republic as a whole. The WIC was far less successful, for so many reasons that its relative failure was perhaps overdetermined, but chiefly because the Iberian powers were much less vulnerable in the Americas than in Asia and there was no equivalent here of the array of oriental products which brought such a profit to the VOC. Apart from furs from North America, about the only things America produced that Europe wanted were silver and sugar – the chief sources of the former were in the Mexican and Bolivian highlands and the Dutch could only act as predators on the Spanish treasure fleets, while the lure of the latter drew the WIC into its doomed Brazilian enterprise. In the end the company had to be refounded and satisfy itself with a leading role in the slave trade.

One of the problems for the WIC was that it was partly founded (in 1621) to attack the American sources of Spanish power, and the conflict between strategic and commercial ends was a constant source of weakness. The VOC was much more single-minded in its pursuit of profit, and this explains much of its success; the Dutch were not out to found colonies in the East but to trade. That they eventually ended up controlling much of Indonesia and Sri Lanka was an unintended, and to some extent regretted, consequence of the needs of commerce.

The Dutch Republic can be regarded as the first modern or capitalist society, as long as certain reservations are kept in mind. Firstly, the transformation of the Dutch economy was largely restricted to the maritime region, and primarily Holland; and, secondly, to some extent the 'modern' economy was the old urban system writ large. The integration of all aspects of the economy through the penetration of market forces, produced a society that was a sharp contrast to the rest of contemporary Europe, and foreshadowed the economic and social shape of the nineteenth century.

This modern society with its high degree of urbanisation, dependence on trade, and commercialised agriculture only spread to the land provinces of the Republic to a limited extent; they were strongly affected by the dynamic influence of the economic development and market opportunities taking place in Holland, but their response was complex, to some extent traditional, and defensive. In most respects they resembled the rest of Europe rather than the new society which was emerging in the maritime regions. There is also a clear line linking seventeenth-century Holland with the early economic successes of Bruges, Ghent and Antwerp,[34] and perhaps the towns of the province taken together can be seen as a single metropolis and the province's boom as the acme of urban capitalism. However, more is involved here than a mere expansion in scale of the old urban economies of the Low Countries: at a certain stage such expansion becomes something qualitatively different, and by the middle of the century something new in the history of the world had emerged in this small area of north-west Europe.

The area thus transformed was limited, however, and the whole phenomenon remained vulnerable to economic forces which it could barely understand and certainly could not control. The expansion of the town economies of the maritime region of the northern Netherlands produced a capitalist society before industrialisation, but its geographical extent was very limited and it was deeply embedded in a European economy which ran on rather different lines. Similarly, it can be said that this economic transformation produced a bourgeois society, at least in the province of Holland, but that this was a bourgeoisie *manqué* – lacking direct political control and still to a large extent in the thrall of a culture which was the product of a very different society.

3

REPUBLICANISM IN PRACTICE

The Dutch Republic has had a bad press in one respect at least: the seventeenth century may have been a golden age in culture and an outstanding success economically, but the Dutch political arrangements of the time have not been admired. The central government is regarded as being so weak a system and so torn between competing provincial interests that it could hardly hold the state together, let alone pursue effective national policies. There have been two main strands to this criticism: Dutch nationalist historiography of the nineteenth and early twentieth centuries, and historians who have taken the centralising, absolutist state as the norm for the early modern period and have seen more traditional systems as anachronistic and necessarily doomed. The newly founded Kingdom of the Netherlands of the nineteenth century needed to justify its existence in opposition to the memory of the greatness of the Republic, and it did so by claiming that the centralised state and monarchy expressed the needs and interests of the Dutch nation far better than the fragmented Republic, where all-powerful provincial egotism had triumphed over national purpose. Such attitudes were reinforced by an interpretation of early modern European history which saw any resistance to absolutism as outdated and inefficient. From either point of view the political system of the Dutch Republic was an anomaly.[1]

One problem is that the Republic does not fit neatly into any of the available – then or now – categories of state. It called itself a republic[2] and vaunted its republican freedoms, but for long periods it was governed by princes of Orange whose powers seemed to be at least quasi-monarchical. So it can be argued that it did not work as a republic and needed the injection of central leadership which only the princes of

61

Orange could give, but that the informal nature of their authority meant it could only function imperfectly as a constitutional monarchy. However, it is clear that the Dutch state preserved republican forms and employed republican rhetoric; the whole legacy of the Revolt, which in the interpretation favoured by the regents in the seventeenth century had been a defence of traditional rights against absolutism, sanctified such forms and provided a content for the rhetoric.

It is somewhat difficult to pin down what the idea of the republic meant to contemporaries. On the simplest level it was purely a negative – a rejection of princely, and especially hereditary, rule. One of the strongest elements of Dutch republicanism across the whole spectrum from unreflecting prejudice to high theory was an aversion to monarchy and an acute awareness of its dangers. This set of attitudes could be and was used to oppose the power of the princes of Orange in the Republic, as being necessarily a threat to fundamental freedoms. However, republicanism also contained positive elements which might perhaps be summed up by the formulation that Dutch burghers were citizens not subjects. The political system was seen as protecting individual freedoms and property against arbitrary acts of government and especially against taxation without consent. Of course, this was not a democratic system – and republicanism in no way implied this – and the rule of oligarchs and nobles could be oppressive, but a republican system was seen as having very important practical consequences. As the publicist Elie Luzac averred in the mid-eighteenth century: 'J'aime bien mieux une République, contente de ses possessions, ne cherchant qu'à les conserver, et à procurer à ses habitants une vie tranquille et paisible.'[3] Republics were seen as fundamentally different from monarchies, with different values and thus different policies. They were not egalitarian: republican freedom embodied the rights and privileges of towns, nobles and other corporate groups, not of all individuals; but the citizens of the towns, for example, shared in such privileges, and communal self-government was more than an abstract ideal for them.

Despite this firm commitment to republicanism in theory, and this practical attachment to local and group rights and privileges, the princes of Orange were able to establish themselves as effective heads of the government of the Republic, with powers that seemed little short of princely, for a substantial proportion of the seventeenth century. From 1618 until the end of the century the dominance of the princes was only interrupted by the first stadhouderless period (1650–72). Sir William Temple made an interesting distinction between the sovereignty of the states (i.e. the representative bodies in each province) and the authority of the princes of Orange.[4] Leaving aside the question whether the states really were sovereign – and if so which states – this formulation focuses attention on the peculiar nature of the power and influence of the princes. Formally the princes were subject to a superior authority in all their offices: as stadhouders to the states of the respective provinces, as head of the army and navy to the States General. On the basis of these positions, however, they were able to build up considerable independent political power.

One of the explanations for their rise to dominance was their ability to provide leadership in war and decisive action at times of crisis, and thus to make up for the military inexperience of civilian politicians, and to represent a counterweight to the notorious indecisiveness of the Republican system. Another aspect of their authority was their ability to exploit the latent power of their offices, and the patronage possibilities which they offered. The provincial stadhouderships proved particularly fruitful in this respect as, however irrational it may have been, they retained some of the powers which their predecessors, the provincial governors, had exercised as representatives of the sovereign before the Revolt. A third element in the influence of the princes is more difficult to assess but should not be underestimated: the charisma which attached to the House of Orange. The heads of the house were independent princes in their own right; as descendants of Willem of Orange they inherited to some extent the prestige of the 'father of the fatherland'; and in a curious way they came to be seen as champions of the Reformed Church and of the calvinist identity of the Republic. In addition each successive prince benefited from the achievements of his predecessors, and the Orange myth grew measurably in the course of the century.

Nevertheless, the final power in effect remained with the states – but not, as might have been expected, with the States General, but with the States of Holland, and it was this body which guaranteed the continuing integrity of the republican system. The States of Holland could be manipulated but not coerced, and their financial strength meant that their consent was essential to the successful government of the Republic. Thus while the princes were able to employ a combination of their formal powers and their patronage systems to control most of the smaller provinces, and particularly their votes in the States General, the towns of Holland were always able to retain at least an essential remnant of independence. At another level it can be said that the republican system survived the dominance of the princes because, even at their most powerful, they had to rely on the cooperation of local power holders. The regents and other local notables had to be allowed what amounted to virtual autonomy at the grass roots; the princes could control only those areas which were not of immediate concern to them.

More fundamental than the uncertainty as to the nature of the Dutch state is the question whether it was a real state at all. Conventionally, the modern state has been associated theoretically with the concept of sovereignty and practically with the strengthening of central government. The Dutch polity had a central government so weak as to be hardly recognisable from this point of view, and the location of sovereignty was so uncertain as to suggest that the term was simply inapplicable. There are both normative and anachronistic assumptions lurking in such criticisms: one form of the modern state is taken as the only viable one, and is used as a criterion by which the Republic can be condemned. Less obviously anachronistic but still radically misleading is to take one form of political thought – that recommending the absolutist and centralising state – and to judge contemporary polities by its standards. Inevitably, this approach leads to the judgement that all traditional, republican and decentralised systems were inefficient, outdated and – in one way or another – doomed.[5] The Dutch Republic is a fine example of such rather messy systems and was criticised by contemporaries who took the centralised, monarchical state as the norm, and by later commentators who have failed to see how it could possibly have worked.

Certainly, the responsibilities – never mind the powers – of the central government of the Republic were minimal: formal control of relations with other countries, the running of the armed forces, and general oversight of common finances (which were almost exclusively concerned with the armed forces). The provinces were in theory almost completely autonomous, and in practice governed themselves. There was not even a central court of law for the Republic as a whole.[6] However, the state held together, despite severe internal strains and constant external pressure, for over two hundred years and only collapsed – along with most of the rest of Europe's *ancien régime* – when faced with the French revolutionary armies. A sense of the union between the provinces as being indissoluble developed quite quickly in the early seventeenth century, and in the long term a sense of unity and perhaps even of national identity – though this is more questionable – grew within the borders of the Dutch state. Admittedly, this sense of unity fell far short of the criteria of nineteenth-century romantic nationalism, but perhaps so much the better.

Above all the Dutch state was successful. It weathered the difficult times of the seventeenth century with considerably less internal disturbance than most monarchies of the time, however much they may have been praised by contemporary theorists. It also proved capable of pursuing an effective and consistent foreign policy, despite the apparent irrationalities of its decision-making processes. Johan de Witt complained to Temple of the wild and, to him, unpredictable fluctuations in English foreign policy throughout the early seventeenth century;[7] this was not the way the Dutch conducted their affairs. The reputation of the Dutch state has suffered for its all-too-evident weaknesses in the eighteenth century; the equally obvious successes of the previous century have tended to be overlooked. The Dutch polity had severe problems, as will become apparent, but for much of the seventeenth century it worked, both in terms of surviving internal crises without breakdown, and of running the country effectively. In these respects it compares favourably with the theoretically more viable absolutist states of the period.

The Dutch Republic cannot properly be understood in terms of conventional thinking about the nature of the state. Even contemporaries found the Dutch state difficult to pin down because they tended to think of political units in terms of the scope of the legal jurisdiction of central authorities, usually individual rulers though collective bodies such as town governments or assemblies of estates could also perform this function. The central authorities of the Republic were so limited in their powers, however, as to bring into question whether it was a state at all in conventional terms. It is probably misleading to take this perspective, and to describe the Dutch state in terms of the decentralisation of political power, as it never had a strong central government which could be seen as defining the state. Political authority was more clearly established at local and provincial levels, and the nature of the Dutch polity was determined by the degree to which circumstances induced or compelled these bodies in practice to cede powers to a central government. The Republic was unique not in having this type of political system – the Swiss Confederation and the Holy Roman Empire[8] can be seen as working polities with similar characteristics – but in managing to be a major power in Europe and the world at the same time.

Contemporaries believed that traditional, republican polities were all very well, but were doomed in an age of increasingly powerful centralised states, and such views have been echoed by modern historians.[9] Normally this was true, but the Dutch Republic, for a while at least, proved to be an exception.

In practice the scope of the central government in the Republic was very limited, and the provinces had a degree of autonomy approaching sovereignty. At the centre of Dutch government was the States General, which was composed of the representatives of each of the seven provinces.[10] Each province had a single vote in the deliberations of this assembly and the provincial delegations were not plenipotentiaries but, in theory at least, bound by the decisions of their principals. In important matters, unanimity was deemed to be necessary, though it was not always possible in practice to hold to this rule. The States General dealt with the foreign relations of the Dutch state, its military and naval affairs, and the administration of the Generality lands; other functions of government were carried out at provincial, or even local, level, and even in the case of the judicial system there were no central courts of justice – on those occasions when a trial under the auspices of the States General was held a special court had to be convened, and its legality was always open to challenge.[11]

The precise relationship between the Generality and the provinces was never entirely clear or, rather, there were competing visions of the constitutional position, neither of which quite fitted the practice. Perhaps the dominant and certainly the most coherent interpretation took as its starting point the essential autonomy of the provinces, and regarded the powers of the Generality as being delegated to it by them and as being in principle revocable. Whether this position necessarily implied absolute sovereignty for the provinces is disputable: it was possible to combine it with a commitment to the Union which in an important sense overrode provincial independence. What is clear is that the Republic would have been almost impossible to govern if the principle of complete provincial autonomy had always been strictly adhered to. Unanimity was necessary in theory, but in practice the opposition of one or more provinces could be overridden – most notoriously when the States of Zeeland refused to ratify the treaty of Münster in 1648 – especially if one of the lesser provinces was concerned. It was an entirely different matter when Holland's opposition (and that of Utrecht) in the States General to commissioning Maurits to enforce the disbandment of the *waardgelders* (hired troops)[12] was overruled in 1618. Here it was clear that the normal rules were being broken in order, in the view of Maurits and his supporters, to avoid worse; the legal justifications the Orangists found for their actions were politically necessary but not serious contributions to Dutch constitutional theory.[13] As soon as the crisis had passed, the theory – and practice – of provincial autonomy was able to reassert itself, and the next time that Holland's veto was overruled by a majority of provinces was in the context of another crisis in the Dutch state. Indeed, the very fact that the military budget of 1650 was accepted in spite of Holland's opposition was a sign that normal political procedures were already breaking down, and was a major step towards the attempted *coup* by Willem II, which itself cannot be seen as anything other than unconstitutional. The death of the prince in the same year allowed for a peaceful resolution of the crisis involving an even more explicit assertion of the principle of provincial independence. However, given that the *Grote Vergadering* convened by Holland in 1651 declared mutual loyalty to the Union, this was possibly not quite the same as full sovereignty and the ambiguity over this issue was never entirely resolved.

The other chief interpretation of the political system of the Republic took as its starting point the effective indissolubility of the Union, and was ready to accept the implications of this for provincial autonomy that the other tradition was reluctant to recognise. However, it was not just a matter of assigning a degree of sovereignty to the States General: this can be seen as a specifically Orangist theory, as it also involved recognising that the princes of Orange, as stadhouders of most provinces and as heads of both army and navy, were an indispensable part of the government of the state. The belief that the central authorities of the Republic must possess powers which in some sense overrode those of the provincial states seems to have been necessarily associated with the idea that the princes of Orange constituted an important part of this central government. Perhaps rightly, it seems to have been considered that the Generality was unlikely to be able to act effectively without the guidance of an 'eminent head'. Thus, while the stress on provincial autonomy led in practice to the predominance of Holland in the politics of the Republic, the more centralist theory involved the princes of Orange becoming the effective head of government.

However, concentration on the question of provincial autonomy disguises the fact that the power of the provincial governments was also limited by semi-autonomous towns and regions. Everywhere the essential location of political authority was at the local rather than the provincial level, though the nature and extent of decentralisation varied from province to province, and a distinction can be made between the more integrated western provinces and the much looser political structure of the land provinces.[14] Gelderland and Overijssel were both formally subdivided in three 'quarters', each with their own representative bodies, and their provincial institutions were relatively weakly developed. In Overijssel the leading towns (Deventer, Kampen, Zwolle) continued to claim the status of imperial cities[15] and were reluctant to recognise the superiority of their provincial government. In Groningen (aptly termed *Stad en Lande*), the division between the town of Groningen and the surrounding countryside was similarly sharp, with the latter having a separate representative assembly. Disputes over competence and clashes of material interests were the order of the day, and provincial unity was fragile at best.

The maritime provinces had much greater provincial coherence. In Holland especially the towns had found that they needed to work together to gain their ends, and had consequently developed an effective provincial government even before the Revolt.[16] Nevertheless, even here power lay with the towns as a body rather than the provincial states. The regents of the towns represented in the States of Holland controlled its actions, and in important matters unanimity was necessary; in theory towns could not be forced to accept decisions to which they had not consented. To a considerable extent, the towns were free to run their own affairs with the minimum of intrusion from the centre. This was notably the case in judicial matters where it was often difficult for the provincial law courts to enforce their decisions on recalcitrant towns. Throughout the Republic local government in both town and countryside had a considerable degree of competence and independence. Communities were largely self-governing with distinctly limited interference from above: in Holland small towns and villages had their own governments, and in the land provinces local administration, though very different in structure, also enjoyed considerable autonomy. On the other hand, the ability to play a part in provincial politics was much more restricted. In general, the provincial states were composed of representatives of the towns and the nobility, but not all towns were represented, and in most provinces noble representation too was in the process of being restricted to an élite, usually in the form of a *ridderschap* with strict rules of membership.[17] In Friesland participation in provincial politics in the countryside was in theory considerably more widespread but was in practice increasingly limited by the manipulation of the system by rural and urban élites; in Groningen the rural notables were perhaps not a conventional noble group but became an increasingly closed oligarchy.[18]

The political system of each province had individual characteristics but, fascinating as such a study might be, these cannot be pursued here. Holland does deserve special attention because of its size, wealth and political influence: the politics of the Republic cannot be understood without an understanding of how power was distributed and decisions made in Holland. It can also serve as an example of the way in which provincial politics worked at this time; the elements – states, regents, nobles – were more or less the same as in the other provinces, though their relative weight and interplay were different. Holland shows a complex relationship between the local and the provincial, and between the various privileged groups and individuals, and in that it was wholly typical of Dutch *ancien régime* politics.

After over a hundred years of economic expansion, Holland contained around 40 per cent of the population of the Republic and probably over 60 per cent of its wealth in the late seventeenth century. This preponderance of one province was already evident in the decades after the break with Spain and posed major problems for the emerging Dutch political system. Holland's financial strength made it possible for it to give political leadership to the other provinces, but the formal equality of the allies meant that each province had the same single vote in the States General. Holland clearly could not let itself be outvoted by a majority of the other provinces, and so required a veto: thus the stress on provincial autonomy was in part a consequence of Holland's need to make its financial weight felt in the new state. Its veto meant that it could not be made to pay for policies it did not support, while its financial power gave it the leverage to persuade the other provinces to follow its lead. The price to be paid for this was twofold: firstly, every province and not only Holland had to have a veto, and the internal politics of all provinces had to be largely free from interference from the centre. The great disparity between Holland and the rest was a prime reason for the far-reaching decentralisation of the Dutch political system.

This end, however, was reached not so much through rational argument and the open discussion of conflicting interests as through the manipulation of tradition. In theory nothing new was being created in the setting up of the Dutch polity, rather a political practice which was conceived as stretching back to antiquity was being rescued from deformation by illegitimate Spanish actions. In consequence, any attempt to meet immediate problems had to be presented as part of the ancient freedoms rather than as a pragmatic innovation. The rights of the states, of the towns and of the nobles could be justified by precedent, but no discussion as to the proper political relationship between towns and the States of Holland could be carried on in any other terms. As we shall see, one of the results of this reliance on precedent and history was that the position of stadhouder retained a political potential despite its redundancy.

Holland was the dominant province throughout the century – indeed throughout the history of the Republic – through its economic and demographic strength. This dominance could take two forms: open leadership of the state, or a sort of powerful constitutional check on the quasi-monarchical authority of the princes of Orange. Holland took the lead in the constitutive years of the Republic; from the departure of Leicester in 1588 to the *coup* by Maurits in 1618, Oldenbarnevelt as *Advocaat van den Lande* of the province was the effective head of the Republic's government. Similarly, during the first so-called stadhouderless period (1650–72), Johan de Witt as *raadpensionaris* (grand pensionary) was the dominant figure in Dutch politics; and in the second stadhouderless period (1702–47) Holland again took the lead. When the government was effectively in the hands of a dominant prince of Orange – as it was from 1618 to 1650 under successively Maurits, Frederik Hendrik, and Willem II, and again from 1672 to 1702 under Willem III – the States of Holland was still a decisive force in the political system of the Republic. Holland's financial strength made its support essential to government, and the principle of provincial autonomy meant that such support could only come through consent. A favourable vote by Holland's delegation in the States General was necessary if any initiative of the stadhouder was to be accepted and paid for; in consequence a vital part of the political task of any prince of Orange was to gain the support of the States of Holland in one way or another.

The formal influence of the province in the central government of the Republic came primarily through its delegation to the States General, where the requirement of unanimity made its single vote crucial. The multifarious business of the States General was conducted through a series of committees and a representative of Holland also sat on every one of these. It also had a strong delegation to the Council of State but here it lacked a formal veto, so this body was less useful as a way of exercising its power.[19] In practice less formal systems were probably more important: the dominance of Oldenbarnevelt and De Witt, for example, worked through a combination of *ad hoc* commissions rather than the explicit powers of their office. Both were the chief officials of the States of Holland,[20] and thus in principle subordinate to the regents who were the real politicians,[21] but they were able to become the leading political figures in Holland and, through their membership of the province's delegation to the States General and appointment to all the important committees, to gain effective control of the government of the Republic as a whole.

At other times Holland's influence was less obvious but, nevertheless, it remained impossible to govern the Dutch state without the cooperation of its leading province. The highest political instance in the province was the States of Holland, but real authority lay in the collective hands of the regents of the leading towns. The towns of Holland may have learned the necessity of working together, but not at the cost of sacrificing urban autonomy in the cause of provincial solidarity. Important decisions in the States required unanimity, formally at least, and it was very difficult in practice to impose central decisions on dissident towns. In an important sense Holland was governed not by the States but by the regents of the leading towns as a group; each town's delegation to the States was strictly bound by the instructions of its principals, the government of its town.

The composition of the States expressed and reflected the domination of the towns: 18 towns and the *ridderschap* (the nobility) each with a single vote.[22] This meant that the nobility were heavily outvoted by the towns, though their prestige possibly gave them more influence than this might suggest, and they were always represented on important committees and in the Holland delegation to the States General.[23] An even more fundamental problem was that, despite their great differences in size and importance, all the towns had the same weight in theory in the States. This meant that towns with only a few thousand inhabitants such as Monnikendam or Purmerend were formally placed on the same footing as towns ten times their size. At the other extreme, Amsterdam with almost 200 000 inhabitants by the late seventeenth century and thus three times as big as Leiden and four times the size of Rotterdam, the next biggest towns, nevertheless had only one vote in the States. However, Hollanders were prepared to be more realistic in everyday practice than in theory; the smaller towns generally accepted the leadership of the larger, and if not and they were isolated they could be swept aside. Similarly Amsterdam was usually accorded something like the respect its wealth required, if not always what its regents felt was its due. Difficulties remained nonetheless, and some of the major political conflicts in the province during the century can be attributed at least in part to Amsterdam feeling that its voice and interests were not receiving proper consideration.[24] The defeat of Oldenbarnevelt and the majority in the States of Holland who supported him in 1618 was only possible because Amsterdam was on the other side, and the latter's adoption of a contraremonstrant position – wholly untypical of either its usual stance on religious issues or the relationship between church and civil magistrate in the town – was to a significant extent a reaction to the way in which the town's views had been flouted over the signing of the truce with Spain. Conversely, Willem II's attempted *coup* in 1650 foundered in the face of a Holland united under the leadership of Amsterdam.[25] Its economic power enabled Amsterdam to give effective leadership to the towns of Holland, but if its interests were not given what its regents believed was proper consideration then the political system of the province could break down.

Although the government of the province was effective, especially in relation to external policy, it was nevertheless restricted in its scope by the large degree of autonomy enjoyed by the towns. Town governments had a wide range of administrative powers and competence, but more importantly it was very difficult in practice for the central authorities of the province to act against them. The problem was that the towns were part of the highest political authority in the province rather than being subject to it, and in any case no town wanted to allow a precedent to be set which might be used against itself at some point in the future. So, although there were appeal courts for the province – the Court of Holland and the High Council[26] – they regularly had difficulty in enforcing their judgements on the towns. There were few effective restrictions on the power of the urban oligarchies, and their legal powers over their citizens were considerable. However, what might be considered almost absolute powers were checked by their lack of instruments of coercion and by their reliance in matters of public order on civic militias recruited from the middling groups in society. In the end some degree of assent from the ruled was necessary, and the citizens could not be pushed too far.[27]

The political role of the princes of Orange in the Dutch Republic is difficult to pin down with any precision. Foreign contemporaries often read their own political circumstances into that of the Dutch and saw the princes as more or less rulers of the country, though with somewhat limited powers, and there is evidence that at least some Dutch contemporaries shared this misapprehension. (Given the complexities of the Republic's system of government it is hardly surprising that many contemporaries had only a rather vague understanding of just how things worked away from the local level.) There was sharp disagreement at the time as to whether the princes were necessary for the efficient running of the state or were a standing threat to the fundamental liberties of the Republic, a dispute which reached a climax perhaps in the pamphlet war of the 1660s.[28] Some historians have seen them as the representatives of the interests of the Dutch nation against the forces of provincialist egoism, though this line of argument is weakened somewhat by doubts as to whether a Dutch identity existed in any real sense before the late eighteenth century at the earliest.[29] Also the concept of national interest was and is difficult to define and open to partisan interpretation. More interesting, perhaps, are the ways in which the princes of Orange were able to manipulate their ambivalent situation into one of great and sometimes nearly monarchical power in the Republic.

The authority of the princes was neither fixed nor given from the start, but changed and developed in the course of the seventeenth century – and was to experience further change in the later part of the eighteenth. The peculiar position of the house of Orange was established by the crucial role played by Willem of Orange in the Revolt: for over a decade he was effectively the political leader of the rebel northern provinces and was on the verge of becoming count of Holland and Zeeland when he was assassinated. His son Maurits was for decades head of the Dutch army but politically overshadowed by Oldenbarnevelt, until his *coup* in 1618 brought him to power. From then on successive princes were the effective heads of government until the end of the century, with their dominance only interrupted by a stadhouderless period from 1650 to 1672. To some extent their power was based on princely prestige and historically developed charisma: they had the status of independent princes (derived from Orange in the Rhône valley), and the reputation of Willem I as 'father of the fatherland' was augmented by Maurits' actions in 1618–19 which were represented as saving the Republic from collapse into civil war, and crowned by Willem III coming to the rescue in 1672 when the Dutch state was apparently at the mercy of Louis XIV's invading army.

Although Maurits' lifestyle was notably modest, his successor Frederik Hendrik encouraged the development of a court round him and lived in a princely style, deliberately perhaps allowing appearances to blur the distinctions between his situation and that of a real ruler. This strategy was followed by his son, Willem II, and grandson, Willem III, and many contemporaries, less aware than legally trained regents of the precise nature of their position, may have been ready to take appearance for reality, and regard the princes as the rulers of the Republic which they never were. Such confusions were encouraged by the fact that some of the powers which attached to the post of stadhouder appeared to be properly only the attribute of a sovereign. From the 1590s the princes of Orange held the stadhouderships of most of the provinces:[30] under the Habsburgs these were provincial governorships and, although the abjuration of Philip II removed any constitutional logic from these positions, power of precedent meant that they continued into the Republican period, and that their powers remained the same. For example, they retained the authority to intervene in the selection of town magistrates, although this derived from their previous position as representative of the sovereign and should have ended when they became formally subject to the provincial estates. Such powers gave the stadhouders both considerable political influence and more than a hint of sovereignty; this combination made these posts the bases of the princes' political authority in the Republic.

It can be argued too that there was a practical need, at times of crisis or more generally during wars, for an undisputed leader for the state, an 'eminent head' in the terminology of the time. This would be more plausible if the examples of first Oldenbarnevelt and then Johan de Witt had not demonstrated that firm leadership, even in time of war, could come from other than a prince of Orange. However, both these men were representatives of Holland's dominance within the union, so it may be that opinion in the other provinces was more comfortable with Orange leadership. In any case, there is evidence that by the middle of the century the dominance of the princes was beginning to be seen as a normal part of the political system.[31] This development was interrupted by the first stadhouderless period but picked up again under Willem III. So both the position of the princes and the common perception of that position was dynamic and changing throughout the century, and this continued to be the case in the following century. The authority of any particular prince of Orange depended on his ability to manipulate the potentialities, both official and informal, of his various offices and positions, and so varied considerably with the personality and capacity of each, as well as with the political circumstances of the time. This makes the assessment of the role of the princes in the Dutch political system more than a little tricky, but an important general trend can be suggested: that their authority increased over time with a certain inexorability. Maurits after 1618 was considerably more powerful than in the earlier part of his career; this position was consolidated by Frederik Hendrik; and – although the combinations of the political errors and early death of Willem II led to a temporary eclipse for Orange – Willem III was possibly even more powerful than his grandfather, certainly his formal authority was greater. Thus the princes were the leading political authority in the Republic for a great part of the seventeenth century – 1618–50 and 1672–1702. They were, however, never formally heads of state and certainly never rulers of the country; their influence came from their position as stadhouders in a majority of the provinces and as leader of the army, usually with the title of captain-general. From Maurits onwards the Orange princes were stadhouders of Holland, Zeeland, Utrecht, Gelderland and Overijssel, and Frederik Hendrik also began to make inroads into the position of the Fries branch of the family as stadhouder in the other provinces.[32] This office varied in power and influence from province to province – and from time to time – and in general it can be said that the stadhouders were stronger in the land provinces and in Zeeland than in Holland, though even here the potential of the post was considerable. In particular, the stadhouders could exercise considerable influence over appointments at all levels, and thus build up a formidable clientele. In Holland, for example, the stadhouder appointed the yearly magistrates (burgemeesters and *schepenen*) from short-lists in most towns, and in some also appointed – again from a short-list – new members of the town councils. Such powers gave the stadhouders the chance to build up a political following in the town governments and thus a strong position in the province as a whole. In Holland the princes were also members of the *ridderschap*, which conferred prestige if perhaps not much else, and in Zeeland as First Noble they controlled this vote in the provincial states.

As member of the Council of State, which had become in effect an executive body of the States General with special responsibility for military affairs, and head of the army (and much less actively of the navy) each prince also had influence on central government, military (and thus foreign) policy, and extensive patronage, particularly as regards commissions in the army. It was this combination of offices and positions, together with the charisma coming from their princely status and the illustrious history of their house, which enabled the princes to become such formidable political operators in the course of the century. This was first signalled in the troubles which arose out of the remonstrant/contraremonstrant split in the Reformed Church during the first decades of the century. By careful manoeuvring and the skilful manipulation of the unrealised potential of his situation, Maurits was able to undermine the position of Oldenbarnevelt and the majority in the States of Holland and eventually seize power. Later princes were able to establish a powerful political hold on the land provinces, a situation that was formalised by the governing regulations (*regeringsre-glementen*) imposed on them under Willem III.

The whole was a curious but potent mix of the traditional powers of the stadhouder – largely anachronistic since the foundation of the Republic but still regarded as legally valid – with extensive powers of patronage and semi-institutionalised charisma. Holland on the one hand represented the tradition of urban power in the Netherlands, but its political culture foreshadowed the new world that was to be created by capitalism and bourgeois rationalism. In contrast, the princes of Orange were the product of traditional forms of power and of a culture still suffused with noble values. Part of their strength in the land provinces came from their ability to work with and through the nobles there, bolstering up their position in provincial politics and at the same time creating a loyal clientele. Culturally too, the nobles and the regents of the rather conservative towns of these provinces were more prepared to accept the leadership of a prince than that of the Holland towns with their ruthless pursuit of their own economic interests. For the smaller provinces, the princes of Orange could represent not so much the nation as a protection from the overweening influence of Holland.

The peculiar religious situation in the Republic provided another variation in the complex relationship of the princes to Dutch political and social life. After Maurits' decisive intervention on the side of the contraremonstrants, the princes of Orange came to be seen as champions of the Reformed Church and especially of reformed orthodoxy, although none of them were particularly pious and at least two – Willem I and Frederik Hendrik – were distinctly hesitant in their relation to calvinism. Willem the Silent's evident *politique* stance did not prevent reformed writers and preachers turning him into a champion of the true faith once he was safely dead, and Maurits' *coup* settled the issue: from then on there was a close alliance between orangism and reformed orthodoxy. Perhaps the ultimate reason for this was the structural clash between the regents – of Holland in particular – and the Reformed Church. The latter had the semi-theocratic urge to impose a single religious standard on the whole of Dutch society, while the regents were much more concerned to maintain social harmony in a religiously divided society. The latter tried to pursue their essentially secularist policies, and to exclude the church from any part in politics; in reaction the Reformed Church tended to look for leadership and support to the Orange stadhouders. Consequently, the more orthodox members of the church tended to form one of the mainstays of orangism, both as practical politics and as a political theory. The princes of Orange could be projected as champions of the traditional ideal that the religious and political communities should be identical although this concept had already – at least to a large extent – become anachronistic. Perhaps the political role of the house of Orange in the Republican period should be seen not as a harbinger of the unified Dutch state under an Orange monarchy of the nineteenth century but as the focus of traditionalist social and religious forces in a rapidly changing society. The princes represented, not the national interest against provincialism, but the weaker provinces against the dominance of Holland; residual dynasticism and noble interests against merchant capitalism; and traditional religious and cultural codes against the pluralist and increasingly secular society that was emerging in the course of the seventeenth century. Seen in this light it is hardly surprising that the princes of Orange in the later eighteenth century proved unable to understand the need for political modernisation, never mind carry it out.[33]

The regents were, as the term implies, those who ruled or rather governed the Republic. In a narrow definition, it is used to indicate the members of the oligarchies that controlled the towns, particularly in Holland. A broader usage would include all those who shared power, such as the nobility and the rural notables in the northern provinces. The Revolt, by eliminating the sovereign, enabled the regents to take over the new state, and in practice this meant that the political élites of the towns extended their influence through the provincial states to the level of the Republic itself. To a considerable extent the Dutch Republic was a collective urban oligarchy, aided and abetted by rural power-holders, and challenged only by the semi-dynastic influence of the princes of Orange. The dominance of the regents was termed 'freedom' and this usage was not entirely hypocritical: the regents, although not democratically elected, were regarded as the embodiment of their communities, and it was this sense of representation which was extended to the level of the state in the Republic, and which was regarded as constituting political liberty. In Holland the regents proper were the oligarchs of the voting towns (i.e. those 18 towns with representation in the States of Holland), and the situation was similar in Zeeland. Elsewhere, however, the situation was more complicated and the regents would have to include the nobles in the *ridderschappen* of the land provinces, and local notables such as the *ambtsjonkers* of Gelderland and the *grietmannen* of Friesland.

The regents of Holland controlled the provincial states and thus to a considerable extent the actions of the States General. They were a closed oligarchy, sitting for life and filling vacancies in their ranks by co-optation. However, they did not form patriciates with a clearly defined membership and there were few formal limitations to prevent outsiders from joining their ranks. In practice, the oligarchies of most of the towns seem to have tended, if left undisturbed, to close up and consolidate power in the hands of a limited group of families, but this process was broken up or slowed down by political upheavals and demographic realities. The regent group had been reconstructed in the course of the rising of 1572 and the immediately succeeding years. This new oligarchy was disrupted in 1618 when the stadhouder carried through large-scale changes in the composition of the governments of the Holland towns (*wetsverzettingen*), and this process was repeated on a similar scale in 1672. There may well have been considerable though less spectacular changes in the ruling groups after the death of Willem II and the institution of the stadhouderless system as orangists, discredited and deprived of support from a stadhouder, proved vulnerable to their opponents, including families thrown out of the oligarchy in 1618. If political upheavals imposed a certain amount of social mobility on the regent group, so did demography. The rapid population growth in the towns increased the pool of those eligible for admittance into the élite, while demographic failure in regent families created openings.[34] Town governments could also be influenced by the stadhouder: after 1618 – with the exception of the stadhouderless periods – and in most towns he appointed burgemeesters and *schepenen* from short-lists, and in some he chose council members (also from a short-list) as well. Just how important these powers were is hard to assess, but the evidence suggests that it was not usual to present the stadhouder with nominations which were wholly unacceptable to him, and that they gave the princes of Orange the ability to build up a following in the voting towns. With the exception of such influence from the stadhouder, as well as the more spectacular but rare *wetsverzettingen*, the town governments were remarkably free from outside interference. The States of Holland and its standing committee, the *gecommitteerde raden*, represented the interests of the towns and were disinclined to challenge their autonomy, while the provincial courts (*Hof*, and *Hoge Raad*) found it hard to impose their decisions on them. Formally the powers of the town governments seem almost absolute but, besides the restrictions imposed by the rule of law, there were practical limitations on what they could do. In the last instance their repressive powers were limited: they depended on the local militia (*schutterij*), recruited from the middling ranks of society, to keep order; so widespread disaffection among respectable citizens could leave the regents in serious difficulties.

In any case, the regents were a separate political group but an integral part of the upper reaches of urban society, and shared its interests, preconceptions and prejudices. This may have changed in the course of the century, and it has been argued that a process of aristocratisation set in which produced a distinct urban political and social élite by the middle of the eighteenth century. On the other hand, it can also be suggested that the regents never really moved very far away from the culture and life-style of the rest of the upper bourgeoisie. Two processes seem to have come together to give the illusion of aristocratisation: firstly, in the course of the seventeenth century the business of government became more time-consuming and regents moved away from direct involvement with trade or manufacture to become full-time politicians; and, secondly, as the economy hit problems in the later part of the century, the regents became more dependent economically on the profits and perquisites of office. In other words the regents became political professionals rather than an urban aristocracy. By the end of the seventeenth century, this professionalisation of the regent group was marked, at least in the larger towns, but there is little evidence as yet to suggest that it was developing into a distinct social order.

The nobility as a whole must be included as part of the regent group in its wider definition. In Holland the nobles had lost much of their power: the *ridderschap* had only one vote in the States of the provinces as against the 18 of the towns and, although they had not lost all influence, politics were dominated by the town regents. In Zeeland, the princes of Orange had taken over the title and position of First Noble, leaving no significant political role for the nobility. In the other provinces, however, the urban regents had at least to share power with the nobles, and in Utrecht, Overijssel and Gelderland the latter were probably more powerful. Here there was formal parity in the states between the towns and the nobility, and much of the countryside was effectively under noble control. The contrast between the near-eclipse of the power of the nobles in Holland and the important part they continued to play in the politics of the land provinces is a further reminder of the profound differences between the leading province and much of the rest of the Republic. Not all nobles shared in this power. In the course of the century a process of oligarchisation took place which concentrated power and profit in the hands of an élite within the nobility: catholic nobles were excluded from power, and eligibility for membership of the *ridderschappen* became progressively more restrictive. The situation in Friesland and Groningen was less straightforward, but here also the political power of noble and non-noble rural notables was very considerable. There was one problem, however, which was shared by the nobles of every province within the Republic: they were dying out. Whether for practical or ideological reasons, no new nobles were created after the Revolt, so demographic attrition steadily whittled away at the nobility. In Holland only 21 noble families were left by the middle of the seventeenth century and by 1730 there were only 6, and in Friesland the number of noble families declined from 58 to 34. By the end of the century this numerical decline was obvious throughout the Republic but no measures were taken to combat it, partly because the surviving nobles benefited from the lack of competition for places of power and profit.

Seventeenth-century politics in the Republic used to be described in terms of a struggle for supremacy between the states-party (or republicans) and the orangists. In recent decades this interpretation has been dismissed as anachronistic and replaced by the study of factional and family interests, particularly at the local level. This latter approach has been very successful in laying bare certain aspects of Dutch political reality, but tends to work on the assumption that political beliefs were irrelevant or no more than disguises for self-interested actions.

However, it is far from self-evident that political beliefs played no part in Dutch politics in the seventeenth century. The analysis of factional struggles is an indispensable tool of the historian, but the influence of political perceptions and ideals must also be brought into the picture. Moreover, the concentration on factions ignores a whole dimension of Dutch political life: the social context in which the regents lived and worked. Dutch society was relatively literate with the most powerful publishing industry in Europe, and political events throughout the century were accompanied, especially in Holland, by a flood of public commentary in books and pamphlets.[35] In these circumstances, a form of public opinion could begin to develop and, although the regents believed that government was their business and their business alone, it could and did have a real influence on the political process.

There were real ideological conflicts in the Republic in the seventeenth century and on at least one occasion, at the height of the remonstrant/contraremonstrant struggle, they were serious enough to threaten civil war. Such disagreements centred on the nature and purpose of the Dutch state, and the Republic was particularly vulnerable to such divisions in the early decades of the century. When the new state had bedded in, such conflicts became less dangerous as they took place within a framework of accepted forms and values. The traditional party labels are a useful starting point. On the one hand were the republicans seeking to preserve and promote the *Ware Vrijheid* (True Freedom), while on the other were the orangists who believed that a strong leading role for the princes of Orange was necessary for the proper functioning of the Dutch state. For republicans, the Revolt had been fought to protect and preserve the ancient liberties of the people of the Netherlands; they regarded provincial and urban autonomy as the essence of these liberties, and princely power as their natural enemy. For more sophisticated elaborations of their ideas they could rely on the classical republican theory of the time, particularly as the Dutch polity could be seen to some extent at least as a coalition of republican city-states. Although Willem the Silent had played a heroic part in the early years of the Revolt, there was already unease at the plan just before his assassination to make him count of Holland and Zeeland. Maurits' take-over of power in 1618 gave new force to such apprehensions. From this point on the power of the princes of Orange was seen by republicans as a potential threat to the integrity of the Dutch political system, and this interpretation was confirmed by Willem II's attempted *coup* in 1650 and by Willem III's undoubtedly autocratic style of government after his rise to power in 1672. In practice, the full republican programme meant the domination of the Republic by the States of Holland, usually led by their *raadpensionaris*.

Despite the suspicions of their opponents, the orangists were not seeking to overthrow traditional liberties and establish a monarchy on their ruins; they believed that the princes provided the Republic with a focus of authority and an effective leadership that it otherwise lacked, but within the republican system. A prince of Orange stood apart from – if not above – the provinces and, in the eyes of the lesser provinces at least, could represent common interests better than any politician from Holland, who would always be suspected of favouring his own province. In practical terms the princes could also provide effective military leadership, demonstrated most impressively by Maurits and Frederik Hendrik, and this was no small consideration given that the Republic was more often at war than not during the seventeenth century. The leadership of the princes could thus strengthen the Dutch state against a hostile world and provide a necessary counterweight to provincial autonomy. Such considerations possibly weighed more heavily in the smaller provinces mistrustful of Holland's hegemony, but there were also powerful forces in the leading province favouring a strong position for the stadhouder.

Another important source of orangist sentiment was Reformed orthodoxy: as has been already noted, the princes could be, and were, seen as the champions of orthodoxy against hostile forces within and without the church. Many calvinists clearly felt that they could not rely on the regents as a group to protect and promote the interests of the Reformed Church. Although in principle all regents had to be members of this church, their political practice was markedly secular in its priorities. There was thus an important religious component in the ideological differences of the time, and this was particularly evident in the early years of the century. To a large extent this seems to have involved a clash between rival conceptions of the nature and purpose of the state: while the traditional view saw church and society as coterminous, the regents found themselves having to deal with a religiously mixed society and in practice evolved an increasingly secular set of political priorities. This underlying difference in perception as to the proper nature of a political community was one of the reasons the religious disputes which came to a head during the Truce with Spain almost led to the disintegration of the Dutch state. Paradoxically, although the orthodox calvinists, supported by Maurits, defeated the remonstrants, the extent to which they could impose their vision on society as a whole in the long term proved limited. Certainly in politics the secular approach of the regents, although not able entirely to suppress religious instincts and reactions, dominated the rest of the century.

In the political world of the Republic in the seventeenth century, access to power was through family and faction rather than party, but this opposition is unhelpful. Faction was not the rival of party but part of its structure, and family and faction could and often did embody ideological values and aims. Political parties at this time were clearly not like their modern counterparts, but there were republican and orangist regents with an awareness of differing and conflicting political ideals. Regent families tended to be the carriers of political traditions, factions were made up of alliances of families, and ideological sympathies were an important element in bringing families together. In this way factions could take on a political colour and begin, alone or with allied factions, to act as parties. There was perhaps a broad consensus within the regent group regarding the proper nature of the political system, but within this general agreement there were important ideological differences not only about individual policies but also as to how the system ought to work. Such conflicts have been played down by recent historians, but they were real enough to contemporaries.

The peculiar character of the Dutch state was a faithful reflection of the nature of Dutch society and its conflicts. The provinces not only enjoyed a considerable degree of autonomy; the distribution of political power within each of them varied with their very different social structures. This congruence between politics and society ensured that the regents – the urban and rural élites – remained loyal, but meant that the central authorities of the state had very limited scope and powers. It has become a commonplace among historians that these circumstances produced a weak state, constantly hamstrung by internal disagreements and incapable of pursuing the interests of the Dutch nation with any efficiency. Such arguments beg the question as to what these interests were, and assume the existence of a Dutch nation at a time when this was at best problematical. Even in the highly centralised modern state it is difficult if not impossible to identify a set of objective national interests, with different parties and pressure groups promoting disparate and often incompatible ends, and the Republic faced acute problems of this nature throughout its history.

There were no natural boundaries to the Republic, in terms of either territory or people. The frontier with the South, for example, was the result of military activities and had no historic, linguistic or cultural justification.[36] To the east historical boundaries were rather more convincing, though even here the *Overkwartier* of Gelderland was denied to the new state, and at times it seemed possible that East Friesland might be absorbed in it. Pieter Geyl spent much of his career arguing for the essential unity of the Dutch-speaking areas of the Netherlands – including, thus, Flanders and Brabant – and, whatever one might think about certain aspects of his argument, the arbitrary nature of the eventual frontier line can hardly be denied. The Republic did not include all Dutch-speaking people, and not all its inhabitants spoke Dutch as their first language – most obviously the Fries speakers. The Generality lands were regarded as colonies to be ruled in the interests of the seven united provinces, and North Brabant's attempts to regain admission to the States General proved futile.[37] Drenthe too, although largely autonomous, was excluded from the States General. Neither territorially nor linguistically was it clear who the Dutch were, and it was only the continued existence of the Dutch state which allowed the development of a consciousness of nationality.

A major problem for the Dutch state was the contrast in size, wealth and interests between Holland and the other provinces. With 40 per cent of the population and nearly 60 per cent of the wealth of the state, Holland could not be expected to bow to the will of the other six provinces, therefore it needed a veto in the States General to protect its own position. Moreover, the rapid growth and international orientation of Holland's economy meant that it had foreign policy concerns that were significantly different from those of its partners. The other provinces, however, also required a high degree of provincial autonomy to protect themselves from being railroaded by the superior weight of the leading province. Holland's veto prevented the States General from overriding its interests, while its financial superiority gave it a very powerful bargaining position. Thus the decentralised system enabled Holland to impose its will on the common policy of the Republic while protecting the internal autonomy of the other provinces.

In these circumstances the fundamental reason for the relative stability of the Dutch state was the dominance of Holland, and this remained true even in those periods when the princes of Orange were able to exercise a semi-monarchical authority in the Republic. Unless Holland consented, a policy could not be formally accepted by the States General; more importantly, no action was practicable unless Holland agreed to pay for it. Even the most powerful of the princes of Orange needed the backing of the States of Holland to be able to pursue their policies: their ability to control the politics of the land provinces and thus their votes in the States General could never be enough, they needed the financial support that only Holland could provide. The princes could wield a great deal of influence in Holland but they were never able to subvert its political system as they were to a large extent able to do in the land provinces. In particular, Amsterdam was an impregnable bulwark of provincial independence throughout the seventeenth century, and the only real defeats the States of Holland suffered during these years were when they were weakened by the defection of their most important member. Oldenbarnevelt's fall in 1618 is a prime example of this truth: if the States of Holland, led by Amsterdam, had been solid in his support it is hard to see how Maurits could have succeeded in bringing him down. Leadership in the Republic alternated between the house of Orange and the *landsadvocaat* or *raadpensionaris* of Holland, but in either case the leading politicians had to work with and through the States of Holland. This provided both a check on the powers of the princes of Orange and the dominant element in the formation of Dutch policies: to a large extent Dutch interests were indeed the *Interest of Holland*.[38]

4

RELIGION, POLITICS AND TOLERATION

The Dutch Republic was notorious among contemporaries for the wide variety of religious beliefs and practices which were permitted on its territory and, although this degree of toleration was generally taken as a sign of the moral degeneracy of Dutch society at the time, it has subsequently been regarded as one of its most admirable traits. It is far from obvious why the Dutch should have ceased – in practice at least – to give as high a priority to religious unity and purity as the rest of seventeenth-century Europe. Conventional wisdom predicted that such religious divisions would inevitably lead to the collapse of political order; the experience of the Dutch state in this century was in the end a practical refutation of this theory – although at the height of the conflict between remonstrants and contraremonstrants in the second decade of the century the opposite must have seemed to be the case. Practical necessity rather than idealism would seem to have been at the root of Dutch toleration at this time; certainly there were distinct limitations on this toleration, and these would seem to have been set equally firmly by the circumstances of the time. The Dutch civil authorities at all levels had only a limited freedom of action: on the one hand, the imposition of religious unity or uniformity was not a practical possibility; on the other, a greater degree of toleration with regard to radical beliefs or to catholic worship was generally regarded as neither desirable nor wise.

In the last years of the sixteenth and the early decades of the seventeenth century, the rulers of the new state were faced with the fact of a religiously divided society. Protestantism had made considerable progress, but for many years the membership at least of the Reformed

Church was distinctly limited and there can be little doubt that it was well into the seventeenth century before even a bare majority of the Dutch population belonged to the official church. Religious conservatives were a numerous though ill-defined category but, if we include all those who were more catholic than anything else, they were probably the largest single group in the country until the middle years of the century. Various protestant sects, particularly mennonites, had significant followings, and there were some areas with strong lutheran movements. Perhaps most unsettling, however, was the uncertainty of the religious situation as a whole. In conventional thought, religion was essential to social and political cohesion, yet a recent study of Haarlem suggests that in the first decades of the seventeenth century something like half the population had no traceable affiliation to any religious group.[1] Although it is not entirely clear what these figures mean, nevertheless if this situation was typical of the Republic as a whole, or even of the towns of Holland alone, the civil authorities had cause for serious concern. If there was no unity of religion to hold the new state together, what could?

Again the conventional answer to this problem was to create religious uniformity by political means, including the use of force if necessary, and indeed a process of confessionalisation throughout catholic as well as protestant Europe has been seen as characteristic of the late sixteenth and early seventeenth centuries.[2] For the Dutch, however, the continuing war for independence with Spain, coupled with the sheer size of the problem of religious nonconformity, made any attempt to impose the Reformed Church on the population as a whole inadvisable. Doubtless, many governments would nevertheless have sought to enforce uniformity, seeing this as a political necessity as much as a religious duty. That the Dutch civil authorities in the main did not follow this line tells us something significant about them as well as about the difficulty of their situation. The regents chose to give a higher priority to domestic order and tranquillity than to religious purity, which might well be seen as a significant step along the path of secularisation.

This was not entirely a matter of choice, as the political authorities lacked effective instruments of coercion. In the decentralised political system of the Republic, there was no single authority which could impose a policy of enforcing religious uniformity on the whole of the Republic; and the local authorities which would have had to put such a policy into effect had neither the will nor the power to do so. The only force available was the army of the state, but even if it had not been fully occupied fighting the war against Spain, any attempt to use it to impose confessional unity would have met with massive resistance at provincial and local levels. Provincial governments jealously guarded their autonomy against central interference, and local authorities were similarly not prepared to accept dictation from outside.

The regents' response to the situation was also influenced by a dislike of religious persecution together with a distrust of clerical power. Such attitudes were partly a reaction to the persecution of protestants in the Spanish period and partly came from the strong erasmian strain in Dutch humanism. The attempts to suppress protestantism in the Netherlands had shown that town governments in particular were reluctant to take action against their own citizens at the behest of the authorities in Brussels, and after the Revolt many regents were disinclined to replace one form of religious persecution by another. A parallel response to the religious troubles of the time was the conviction that force was inappropriate in matters of faith: people could be persuaded but not coerced. Perhaps even more marked in the regent group as a whole was the erastian urge to keep matters in their own hands and resist clerical attempts to dictate the agenda of the civil authorities. It became a cliché of contemporary political discourse not only that the intemperate actions of religious zealots were as likely to endanger the causes they supported as to bring them to fruition, but that they were a threat to social and political stability. The latter point is perhaps the key to an understanding of the actions of the political authorities in this vital area: in the end they were concerned more with the preservation of peace and order within their communities, and with the pursuit of prosperity, than with religious purity. Of course, some of the regents had other priorities, and on occasions some town governments can be found pursuing policies which strongly favoured a rather narrow interpretation of reformed orthodoxy, but in the main the civil authorities in the new state revealed themselves to be not just pragmatic in their methods but essentially secular in their aims in their reactions to the religious problems facing them.

However, toleration could not be complete in this period, even in the Dutch Republic; if there were practical limitations on persecution, equally there were limits to what could in practice be openly tolerated. Partly this stemmed from the attitudes and beliefs of the regents themselves, but more profoundly from the assumptions and norms of the society they had to govern. The regents were believing, practising christians and were in theory – and after 1618 very largely in fact – members of the Reformed Church and this imposed limits on what they saw as morally acceptable – the Catholic Church, for example, was widely regarded as not just in error, but as a tool of the devil, and so even for liberal protestants toleration of catholics was distinctly problematic. In another key area, atheism was seen as incompatible with a civilised society, as it deprived it of its moral foundations. Such attitudes were shared by society at large – though the catholics, for example, would have to reverse some of the polarities – and defined the lines beyond which public policy could not go. In any case, the Dutch regents were not, and could not, be protagonists of a wholly secular policy in a society which continued in the main to define itself in religious terms. Dutch society in the seventeenth century saw a complex struggle between emergent secular values and a deeply rooted religious culture, and both rulers and ruled were involved on both sides of the conflict.

The situation of the Reformed Church was an unusual one for early modern Europe in that it was the official church of the state, but not the state church in the normal sense of the term as the inhabitants of the Dutch state were not required to be members of the new church, or even to attend its services. In most of Europe – in theory at least – the political and religious communities were coterminous, and membership of one implied membership of the other; this identity of political and religious communities was, as we have seen, absent in the Republic from the very beginning. This situation was in part a consequence of the religious diversity of the northern Netherlands in the early years after the Revolt, but during the years of persecution the Reformed Church had seen itself as a gathered church of saints, and the desire to continue as a disciplined and pure community of believers continued into the seventeenth century and made it somewhat ambivalent to the possibility of becoming a church for the whole community if this was at the cost of watering-down the quality of its membership.[3] However, the Reformed Church did become the official church of the new state, and this link was important for both the church and the state.

After the Revolt, the civil authorities took over all ecclesiastical property; the Reformed Church was given the use of the churches for its services, and the income from the property of the old church was used to pay the salaries of its ministers. The ownership of both churches and other property, however, came into the hands of the civil authorities and there it remained: in the towns, for example, the churches were owned by the town governments, and in Holland there was a separate office for the administration of ecclesiastical goods in the province. So the Reformed Church took the place of the old church to an important extent, with its ministers preaching in its churches and receiving salaries from the property it had accumulated over the centuries, but it did not inherit the same position in society. There may have been advantages, social and political, to membership of the Reformed Church[4] but there was no legal coercion and the size of its following grew only slowly in the early decades of the century.

Membership figures are difficult to interpret, as they exclude regular churchgoers who were not full members, and these were probably numerous in the period of uncertainty in the late sixteenth and early seventeenth centuries. There were also considerable differences between provinces, with the progress of the Reformation being hindered by the continuation of military operations in large sections of the land provinces, while the Church could organise itself more rapidly in the better protected provinces – Zeeland, Holland, Friesland. In sharp contrast, the Generality lands remained impervious to protestantism throughout the history of the Republic. In these circumstances, figures for the Republic overall can be misleading, and it is possible that the Reformed Church only became the majority religious group for the country as a whole in the second half of the century. In contrast, in Holland it was probably the most important church by the first decade – though the difficulty about assessing religious affiliations must make any conclusion tentative.

Politically, however, the position of the church was much stronger than these figures might seem to warrant. Although the relationship between the political élite and the church was not always smooth, it was always close. For a considerable period after the Revolt, the regent group included men who were not members of the church and who were at best lukewarm in its support, but the size of this element tended to diminish over time and after the upheaval of 1618, in Holland at least, it became the rule that all holders of public office should be members of the Reformed Church. This relationship was symbolised by the provision of *herenbanken* – special pews for the regents – in the churches, but it was not always harmonious. The civil authorities felt it necessary to keep a sharp eye on the activities of the church and its leaders, in particular to prevent interference in political matters. The provincial states sent observers to synods, and local authorities had a variety of ways of keeping check on the doings of local church councils – often regents would themselves act as elders or deacons, or town governments would send representatives to meetings of the consistory. Also, of course, the *herenbank* could be expected to listen to the sermons preached before them with a sharp ear for subversive content. The selection of ministers was also an area of frequent conflict, with the civil authorities in the main claiming greater influence over such appointments than the church was inclined to allow. Although it would be misleading to overplay this as a source of friction, it never proved possible to cobble together a regulation covering clerical appointments in Holland that was acceptable to both sides; this failure is symptomatic of what was perhaps ultimately an irreconcilable conflict of interest between church and state. The Reformed Church had an organisation which made independence from state control possible. At the base, the local churches were administered by consistories of ministers, elders and deacons; at the next level were regional classes consisting of delegates from the consistories; and the classes in turn sent delegates to provincial synods. The natural top of this system should have been regular national synods, but the synod of Dordt (Dordrecht) in 1618–19 was both the first and the last of the century. The provinces' jealous protection of their own autonomy included ecclesiastical affairs as well, and dictation in such matters by a super-provincial body was regarded as politically unacceptable, except in the grave crisis which brought about the meeting at Dordrecht. This restriction on the church's organisational freedom is a reminder that it was too important to be allowed as much independence as it might have wished: the drawback to its privileged position was that it inevitably led to state interference in its affairs. The civil authorities owned the buildings the church used for its services, they paid the salaries of its ministers, and they shared the erastian instincts of their peers throughout Europe at this time. In most areas where protestantism succeeded it had been introduced, indeed imposed, from above and the government subsequently retained control over the newly reformed church; in the nascent Republic, the process had been much more ambivalent and the church maintained its claim to independence of state control, but political realities and the priorities of government made this an unrealistic aspiration.

The way in which the reformed movement had developed gave the church sectarian tendencies to balance its drive to convert the whole of Dutch society. On the one hand was the urge to make the whole community conform to its own standards of proper belief and behaviour; on the other was the desire to maintain internal discipline and purity. In the end the church was able to embrace a great part of contemporary society, but perhaps at the cost of compromising its own principles. A study of the church court in Amsterdam suggests that as the church's membership became larger, so disciplinary standards became less demanding.[5] Of course, Amsterdam was bigger, possibly badder, and certainly more heterogeneous than most Dutch towns but the problem facing the church does not seem to have been significantly different elsewhere – there was a price to pay for a rising membership.

The conflicts within Dutch protestantism in the years after the Revolt concerned essentially what sort of church was appropriate to the situation in the Republic. Both the so-called libertines of the 1580s and '90s, and the remonstrants later stood for a church which was both broader theologically and less oppressive in its discipline than the rigorists were prepared to accept. Only in this way, it was felt, could religious unity at both local and state level be recreated.[6] The victory of the contraremonstrants in 1618 and at the synod of Dordt in the following year marked the triumph of the rigorists, but this victory was perhaps Pyrrhic; the very success of the public church made it more flexible in its practice and in the end perhaps rather like the church the defeated moderates had envisaged.

Such adaptation to political and social pressures was resisted by the movement towards a further reformation (*nadere reformatie*) in church and society. It had parallels with English puritanism – indeed puritan writings were widely read in translation in the Republic – but the Dutch reformers already had the presbyterian structure which the English were struggling for, and so were free to concentrate on the task of building a godly society. In practice, this came down to the cultivation of personal piety, but the aim of these reformers was to impose their values on society as a whole; although they failed to achieve this unrealistic target, their power as a pressure group should not be underestimated. The most prominent of the prophets of further reformation in the early years of the century was Willem Teellinck, and the cause was given further impetus later by such able publicists as Gijsbert Voet (Voetius), a reformed minister and from 1635 professor of theology at the University of Utrecht. These zealots were a small but highly vocal group, and their influence on public policy was far greater than their numbers might seem to have warranted. However, in the end they were bound to fail: the values and practices of a spiritual élite proved inapplicable to society as a whole. The *nadere reformatie* was an attempt to infuse the Reformed Church with the spirit of the heroic days of persecution, and as such it represented perhaps an anachronistic rejection of the values inherent in the new Dutch society that was emerging in the first half of the century.

The Dutch Republic is often seen as a calvinist, or at least as a protestant, state but it must be stressed that the catholics were always a large proportion of its total population. Their situation was ambivalent: they enjoyed freedom of conscience but not of worship, and in so far as the Dutch state identified itself as protestant, they became increasingly outsiders in their own society. So they were better off than most religious minorities in contemporary Europe, and in practice they were very largely able to evade the laws against the practice of their faith, but they were excluded from politics and public office and had to hide their services behind at least an appearance of secrecy.

Catholic numbers are difficult to assess, especially in the early decades of the century, and regional concentrations of catholic strength can make figures for the Republic as a whole somewhat misleading. The issue has been distorted by the tendency, particularly but not only by catholic scholars, to assume that everyone who was not a signed-up member of a protestant church or sect had to be a catholic. The truth would seem to be that convinced catholics and protestants were both minorities in the early decades of the Republic's existence with the majority being indifferent or undecided. The almost complete organisational collapse of the Catholic Church in the northern Netherlands after the Revolt left those who might well have been more catholic than anything else bereft of spiritual leadership; there was widespread nostalgia for traditional practices but little in the way of an understanding of, or a more positive commitment to, what the church stood for. Only with the slow but steady organisation of a catholic mission-church in the Republic in the first half of the century did it become possible to determine who was and who was not catholic. The presence of mission priests enabled – and often perhaps forced – individuals to determine their religious identity; and contemporary records begin to make plausible estimates of church membership possible. By about mid century, when this process was more or less complete, about 35–40 per cent of the total population can be regarded as being catholic. However, they were very unevenly spread through the Republic: North Brabant in the Generality lands was almost completely catholic, and there were areas of heavy catholic concentration in the countryside of Gelderland,

Overijssel, Utrecht and even Holland. In contrast, the towns in general were more protestant, and those in Holland, in particular, had relatively low proportions of catholics, probably nowhere above 20 per cent and often below 10 per cent. Thus a high proportion of catholics lived in areas of very limited political clout – the Generality lands and country areas – while the powerful voting towns of Holland were strongly protestant.

Right from the beginning of the Republic it was clear that, despite pressure from some reformed quarters, catholics were going to be allowed freedom of conscience. In the context of contemporary Europe, where it was normal for the law to be used to enforce conformity to the state church, this was an unusual degree of tolerance, but it did not include freedom for catholics to practise their faith, at least in public.

Moreover, the tone of public pronouncements was decidedly anti-catholic: throughout the century, the civil authorities at every level continued to pass strongly worded *plakkaten*, laws and regulations against the activities of catholics and the catholic church as an affront to god and a threat to the godly society. In fact, the limits on catholic freedom of worship were much less severe in practice than in law, and the situation seems to have improved more or less steadily in the course of the century. In the first half of the century the Republic became a mission territory for the Catholic Church, with an apostolic vicar based in Cologne controlling a system of stations manned by regular and secular priests. In these circumstances, lay support for the works of the mission priests was vital and a particularly important role was played by *klopjes*, women with a religious vocation but able to work actively for the church in the world. Secret churches (*schuilkerken*) were set up throughout the Republic though it is doubtful whether they were particularly secret – in town or countryside the existence of places of regular catholic worship can hardly have been kept a secret for long. They survived because the authorities chose to turn a blind eye to them: bribes were paid, undoubtedly, but the chief reason for this benign misconduct seems to have been a pragmatic acceptance of the inevitable. Where catholics existed in any numbers they would want to worship together; as long as they acted with due discretion, local authorities would accept what they had neither the power nor the will to prevent. Yet such arrangements between catholics and their local *schouten* and *baljuwen* – officials with both police and prosecuting functions – could never be publicly acknowledged; however obvious it was to those living nearby that *schuilkerken* existed and that no action was being taken against them, protestant opinion required that the pretence that catholics were beyond the pale be maintained. By the later part of the century there was a ritualistic element to the regular denunciations of the misdeeds of the catholics from the representatives of the Reformed Church and in response the reissuing or strengthening of anti-catholic legislation by the political authorities, yet with both sides knowing that little or nothing would in fact be done. The high degree of autonomy for towns, rural areas and villages everywhere in the Republic meant that such decisions were essentially taken by the local élites. In some areas of the countryside, catholics were just too numerous for a ban on worship to be practical politics, while in others the authorities as usual chose peace and order before religious purity. In any case the notables who controlled politics at this level were determined to resist outside pressure, either from the States General or from their provincial states, and to act as they judged fit for the particular needs of their own communities. There were other advantages to allowing the catholics to organise themselves at the local level: they could then be expected to take a considerable financial burden off local government by looking after their own poor. It has been argued that its control of poor relief was an important factor in inducing people to conform to the Reformed Church, and there may well be a degree of truth in this, but in general the desire to save money was a more pressing concern than the hope of converting catholics.

Nevertheless, despite such a degree of toleration in practice, the catholics remained to a significant extent outsiders in their own country. In the first years of the Republic, catholics – or at least religious conservatives – could still be found among regent groups throughout the country, but as the seventeenth century progressed they were increasingly excluded from government. The crisis of 1618 was perhaps decisive: as the orthodox reformed took a stronger grip on politics the remaining catholics were forced out along with the protestant dissenters. For the rest of the century – indeed, until the end of the Republic – catholics were excluded from any participation in the political life of the state at any level. Not only were they kept out of the regent oligarchies of Holland but, perhaps more surprisingly, catholic nobles were excluded from the *ridderschappen* in the land provinces. In so far as the official ideology of the new state was protestant, catholics were also excluded from full participation in the common aims which were formulated by the political élite.

An important element in the Revolt had been protestant resistance to persecution by catholic authorities, and a protestant myth developed in the course of the seventeenth century which saw this religious aspect as its essential meaning. In this interpretation, the Republic was protestant in origin and identity and had a providential purpose to fight for the true worship of God and the eradication of catholic superstition.[7] This can hardly have been a concept of common purpose which Dutch catholics could make their own. Their exclusion from politics must also have undermined their sense of belonging, not only with regard to the new state but even to their own local communities, especially in areas such as North Brabant where an overwhelmingly catholic population was ruled by a protestant minority, many of whom had been intruded by the States General.

On the other hand, there is evidence that catholics in general were integrated in Dutch society, particularly in the booming and heterogeneous towns of Holland. Though they felt the need to develop their own institutions and these, along with their church's opposition to mixed marriages, may have separated them off from their protestant neighbours to some extent, there were no catholic ghettos: they lived almost literally cheek by jowl with the rest of the population in the crowded urban space with remarkably little apparent friction. There were no anti-catholic riots in Holland in the seventeenth century,[8] and the large catholic community in the Republic does not seem to have provoked the sort of paranoid reaction in the protestant majority that was the response to the comparatively tiny recusant group in contemporary England. So Dutch catholics enjoyed a degree of toleration that was generous by the standards of the time,[9] and in a political system where the great majority of the inhabitants had no part in government their exclusion from it was perhaps not particularly galling. However, the Republic was for all its secularising tendencies a protestant state, and in so far as a sense of Dutch national identity was beginning to grow in this period it too had a marked protestant stamp. Just how Dutch catholics experienced this exclusion is as yet difficult to say but its long-term legacy was a major problem for the modern Dutch state, and the full integration of catholics into national life was perhaps not completed until the second half of the twentieth century.

The situation for protestants who were not part of the Reformed Church was more favourable than for catholics, and they made an important contribution to the intellectual and spiritual life of the

Republic, yet their numbers seem to have declined more or less steadily in the course of the century. Protestant nonconformists had not only freedom of conscience but in practice freedom of worship as well, though there were restrictions on the activities of the more radical individuals and sects. At the beginning of the seventeenth century, the largest of these dissenting groups was formed by the mennonite baptists, though they were weakened by internal divisions, and the lutherans also had local importance in a few places. There is reliable evidence that by the end of the eighteenth century the number of dissenters had declined considerably, but quite when this shift took place is as yet unclear.

The expulsion of the remonstrants from the Reformed Church in 1619 reinforced the dissenters. For a few years they and particularly their ministers suffered persecution from local authorities under the temporary domination of the militant orthodox, but once the remonstrants accepted their exclusion from the Reformed Church the way proved open for them to set themselves up as a separate and tolerated church, and from about the beginning of the 1630s remonstrant churches appeared in various towns in Holland and elsewhere. The importance of the Remonstrant Church lay not so much in the number of its members as in their high social profile and the intellectual eminence of its leading ministers. The new church drew a high proportion of its members from the better educated and wealthier sections of the population – though as nonconformists they were formally excluded from political office, of course.[10] Their college in Amsterdam quickly achieved a high academic reputation, and remonstrant theologians from Episcopius to Le Clerc gained European prominence as champions of liberal protestant thought. The Remonstrant Church had a high status socially and its theology, although more liberal than orthodox calvinism had become, was at the distinctly respectable end of the dissenting spectrum.

The greatest losses in numbers in the course of the seventeenth century were suffered by the mennonites. In the late sixteenth century they could be seen as serious rivals to the Reformed Church through the austerity of their life and the rigour of their discipline, but their tendency to split up into ever smaller feuding groups together with the seductions of conformity to the official church weakened the movement. By mid century the mennonites had become a numerically small, though intellectually lively, sect which could no longer be seen as a threat to the established position of the Reformed Church. The reasons for this erosion of baptist support are largely unexplored, and it remains a particularly puzzling aspect of the variegated religious life of the Republic. Perhaps their strict moral code was unlikely to attract more than a small minority in the exuberant atmosphere of the Republic's boom years. In any case the religiously or socially discontented began to be attracted to newer and apparently more dynamic radical groups.

The appearance of new sects and new heterodoxies testifies to the continuing dynamism of Dutch religious life in the seventeenth century, but the numbers attracted to such groups were always small and they could not halt the steady advance of the Reformed Church throughout the Republic. The collegiants, for example, were an indirect result of the persecution of the remonstrants after 1619 but, starting from a series of meetings by dissenters at Rijnsburg near Leiden, they became one of the more distinctive, if not bizarre, religious groups of the century.[11] They were not a church or a sect as they had no dogma and no formal membership; the colleges held no services, but their meetings were open for discussion and the expression of beliefs and religious experiences. The movement spread throughout Holland and attracted people from a wide range of social backgrounds and religious directions, from mystically inclined calvinists to rationalist liberals, but catholics were excluded. They brought to a logical conclusion one aspect of protestantism which had inevitably been sidelined in the process of setting up the new protestant churches: individual freedom of judgement and interpretation. In particular, competition between the various strands of protestantism and fierce disputes between theologians encouraged narrower and narrower definitions of religious orthodoxy – of which the conflict between remonstrants and contra-remonstrants in the Republic was a particularly telling example – and pressure on individual members to subordinate their judgements to these dogmas. The collegiants made a radical break from this process.[12] The movement seems to have peaked in the third quarter of the century but then to have faded, perhaps because its very beliefs prevented it from creating the institutional structure which could have given it greater longevity.

Various other radical groups, marked by ascetic flight from the world, mysticism and millenarian zeal, also flourished particularly strongly in the decades after the mid century. The most prominent of these were probably the movements led by Jean de Labadie and Antoinette Bourignon, both of which proved capable of attracting

followers from the social and intellectual élite. The influence of Bourignon caused the distinguished naturalist Jan Swammerdam to aban-
don his studies and his career, while the renowned bluestocking Anna
Maria van Schurman also succumbed to the appeal of radical mysticism. In this period also, Pieter Plockhoy developed a form of religious
radicalism with more emphasis on reform of society, but to little practical effect apart from a short-lived utopian community in New Netherland. Similarly, the influence of Descartes' thought in the Republic
played its part in helping to undermine the philosophical basis of
orthodox theology – which was as important in calvinism as in catholicism – and encouraging rationalist critiques of conventional religion.
Whether mystical or rational, however, such movements had too few
followers to weaken the hold of the established churches and, like the
collegiants, these movements seem to have lost much of their élan by
the final decades of the century.

More lasting, perhaps, were movements for change within the
Reformed Church: the *nadere reformatie* continued with an increasingly
pietistic profile, but the dominance of the more narrowly orthodox was
challenged on a number of fronts and with increasing success from about
the 1640s. In the following decade the controversy over the reinterpretation of orthodox positions by Cocceius and his followers set the tone of
dispute within the church for much of the rest of the century, while
Balthasar Bekker's attack on conventional witchcraft beliefs, although it
led to his suspension from his position as minister in Amsterdam, also
revealed the strength of support for his position. Bekker, rather than his
opponents, pointed the way to the rational, moderate calvinism which
marked the Reformed Church in the eighteenth century.

Another group which found in the Republic a tolerance unusual for
the period were the jews. Most lived in Amsterdam, and were able to
build synagogues, worship freely, and organise their community with
the tacit consent of the government of the town. Again, it seems that
such toleration could not be acknowledged public policy, but had to be
developed in practice and by regular verbal, not written, agreements.
For example, the first synagogue was built when there was an official
ban in place, and it is clear that the burgemeesters must have made it
clear that they would take no action.[13]

For the rest of the century, it seems, there were more or less regular
meetings between the leaders of the jewish community and representatives of the government of the town, but nothing was put on paper let
alone announced as public policy:[14] a wide measure of toleration was

achieved by systematically avoiding any confrontation with the sensitiv-
ities or prejudices of churchmen or the christian population in general.
There were, however, limits to the tolerance of the host community,
marked by fears of religious pollution and sexual transgression. The
fear of sexual exploitation of christian women, especially of those in
vulnerable situations such as maidservants, by jewish men led to a
number of laws designed to preserve a sexually watertight barrier
between the two religions. Such deep unease about what was felt as
an alien presence also showed itself in fears that christians might be
seduced from their faith by jewish example or proselytising. The presence of leading jewish scholars such as Menasseh ben Israel in the
Republic gave the opportunity for theologians and linguists to discuss
problems concerning the interpretation of Hebrew and Aramaic texts
and jewish laws and customs, but it also gave a prominence to this rival
tradition which caused grave unease to many.

The jews arrived in the Republic in two main and contrasting waves:
the first, in the last years of the sixteenth century and the first decades
of the seventeenth, was largely composed of sephardic jews of Spanish
and Portuguese origins; the second, of azkhenazim from eastern and
central Europe came in the second half of the century. The first were
mainly Portuguese-speaking, relatively prosperous, and included many
whose families had been forcibly converted to christianity and who
needed to learn what it meant to be jewish. The second wave spoke
Yiddish and came from ghettos and shtetls where their ancient
customs and beliefs had been faithfully and rigidly preserved; they
had been driven from their homes by a series of pogroms and were
often destitute. Their arrival disturbed the relatively respectable position which had been built up by the sephardim; the influx of poor
eastern Europeans with alien manners and customs and whose poverty
threatened to become a burden on the host community was perhaps an
embarrassment. Certainly, the ashkenazim became a much more marginal group in Dutch society, often scraping a living in a variety of
dubious ways, and it is hardly surprising that by the eighteenth century
there had developed a distinctive brand of jewish criminality.[15] It was
much easier for Dutch society to deal with the relatively small, prosperous and to an extent culturally assimilated sephardim, than with the
more numerous, poor and visibly alien azkhenazim.

Within this unusually tolerant atmosphere, it comes as a surprise to
realise that it was precisely religious divisions within the Reformed

Church which precipitated – caused would be too strong a term – the most serious crisis of the century in the Dutch polity. The conflict between between remonstrants and contraremonstrants led to the arrest, trial and execution of Oldenbarnevelt, accompanied by a purge of the ruling élite, and his replacement as leader of the Republic by Maurits. Moreover, for a few years after their defeat, the remonstrants were persecuted with greater ferocity than ever the catholics were. This episode reveals the continuing importance of religion in the Dutch polity and some of the limits to Dutch toleration.

The controversy broke out soon after the appointment of Arminius to a chair of theology at the university of Leiden. He came into conflict with another Leiden theologian, Gomarus, who accused him of deviating from reformed orthodoxy particularly on the issue of predestination. Although Arminius was cautious in expressing his doubts, at least in public, and the points at issue seem somewhat recondite at first glance, in retrospect it is clear that the implications for the nature of the Reformed Church were profound. A central point was that Arminius and his supporters proposed that the Netherlands' Confession and the Heidelberg catechism be reviewed in the light of scripture, while their opponents regarded these documents as unchallengeable statements of the true faith. In essence the arminians were attacking a nascent calvinist orthodoxy in the name of what they saw as a broader protestant consensus. They rejected the narrow predestinarian theology of the gomarists in favour of universal grace where salvation was at least offered to all and the individual had to cooperate in the reception of grace. The attitude of the other camp was later summed up by William Ames:

> Whether the Death of Christ is Intended for Everyone:
> For whom it is intended, to those it is applied.
> But it is not applied to all.
> Therefore it is not intended for all.[16]

In effect, the arminians were arguing for a church that could embrace most of society, as there was at least hope that most might be saved, while the orthodox still looked for a church of gathered saints, defined by strict congregational discipline.

The arminians knew themselves to be in a minority within the church and sought political support to avoid what otherwise would have been an inevitable defeat, and addressed a remonstrance (i.e. petition) to the

States of Holland in 1610 outlining their beliefs and asking for protection, in response to which the gomarists produced a counter-remonstrance, and two new names appeared in the theologico-political vocabulary of the time. The remonstrants were weak in numbers but were strategically well placed: the university of Leiden was the most important source of ministers for the Reformed Church and here their influence was strong, particularly after they gained control of the States College.[17] They could hope to form the theological and ecclesiological thinking of successive generations of newly minted ministers and so eventually change the Church from inside. This situation, together with the political support the remonstrants gained, was what caused the contraremonstrants so much concern; they saw their Church threatened with destruction from within: for them the remonstrants represented not a minor liberalisation of doctrine, but a first step on a road which, once trodden, would inevitably lead back to Rome.

The remonstrant movement gained considerable regent support notably, but not only, in Holland, and this gave it the chance to expand despite the strength of its opponents within the Church. However, it also brought the issue into the political arena and subtly changed its nature. One reason why the political élites of the Holland towns were so ready to give their backing to the remonstrants was that they had responsibility for communities which were religiously very mixed, and a doctrinally moderate church seemed more likely to become an effective force for communal unity than one marked by a narrowly defined doctrine and strict congregational discipline. The regents may have been attracted by remonstrant theology, but they were driven to action by what they saw as its ecclesiological implications. Moreover, the erastian instincts of the regents as a whole were hardly satisfied by the ambivalence of the Reformed Church with regard to the authority of the civil power in religious affairs, while the remonstrants, recognising their need for support from this quarter, were eventually willing to give unequivocal recognition to the final authority of the regents. Thus there began a series of struggles at local level, with town governments trying to impose remonstrant ministers on often reluctant congregations, and so provoking considerable popular unrest. Not all regents favoured the remonstrants, of course, and in some places the polarities were reversed – Alkmaar in 1610 saw a rising of remonstrant *schutters* against a contraremonstrant town government, for example – but many of the Holland towns went over to the remonstrant side and they were able to build up a powerful lobby in the States of Holland.

However, by about 1611 Amsterdam had moved into the orthodox camp – only partly it would seem for religious reasons – and in the end this was to prove a decisive weakness for the remonstrant cause.

A crisis began to develop when these religious differences at the local level became entangled with more overtly political issues. Oldenbarnevelt – although apparently a contraremonstrant in theological terms – was deeply distrustful of religious extremists and a convinced supporter of Holland's autonomy. Consequently, he was ready to place the contra-remonstrants in the category of those trouble-makers who, he believed, had all too often endangered the state in its brief history. Just as import-antly, once he realised that a national synod was likely to condemn Holland's remonstrants, he took the position that religious matters were an indispensable part of provincial autonomy. The growing antag-onism between Oldenbarnevelt and count Maurits, which first came to the surface over the truce with Spain (1609) and foreign policy in general, brought another line of cleavage within the Republic, and one which to a significant extent coincided with the religious disputes. Differences of opinion over economic policy further complicated the situation: to facil-itate the truce, the formation of a West India Company had been blocked and this alienated a powerful group of Amsterdam regents from Old-enbarnevelt's regime; more generally they were not the only ones to feel disadvantaged by the economic consequences of the Truce.

As these diverse elements came together, the contraremonstrants began to perceive Oldenbarnevelt and his supporters as a threat to the survival of the state. The provinces were held together by an alliance to wage war against Spain, but Oldenbarnevelt had pushed through the truce, which it was feared would leave Spain free to attack again when it best suited her. Adherence to a common religion was also seen as an indispensable unifying factor for the Republic, but Old-enbarnevelt's support for the remonstrants seemed likely to create a religious rift between Holland and the other provinces. In the eyes of his enemies, the Advocate seemed intent on dividing the Republic internally and weakening it externally. The last straw came when in the spring of 1617 he forced the Sharp Resolution through the States of Holland, empowering town governments to take on their own troops to stem civil disorder. This was seen as an attempt to create an army to rival that of the state (led by Maurits) and thus as a preparation for civil war. In the final crisis the position of Oldenbarnevelt and the majority in the States of Holland was fatally weakened by Amsterdam being in the other camp, and in the event Maurits was able to carry out a more or less bloodless *coup*, which brought him to power and cleared the way for the Synod of Dordt to settle the religious dispute.

Inevitably, the synod – which included delegations from most of the reformed churches of Europe – condemned the remonstrants, and its decrees provided a clear and internationally accepted definition of calvinist orthodoxy. Those remonstrant ministers who refused to submit were forbidden to preach, and for a number of years the Republic saw the unedifying spectacle of such men and their supporters being harried by fanatical contraremonstrant regents and police officials. With time tempers cooled, more moderate men returned to power, and one by one the towns of Holland eased off persecution of the remonstrants. Maurits' death and his replacement by Frederik Hendrik, who was much less commited to the contraremonstrants, helped ease the situation, as did the recognition by the remonstrants that they had to accept their expulsion and set up their own church. As a separate church, the remonstrants no longer threatened the integrity of the Reformed Church from inside and, although there were outraged protests from the champions of reformed orthodoxy, the way was open for the remonstrants to be tolerated on a similar basis to the other protestant sects. This whole episode reminds us that even in the tolerant and pluralist Republic some degree of religious unity was felt to be necessary for the survival of the state.[18]

Despite the imperfections of the Reformed Church as a unifying force, especially in the early years of the century when its organisation was weak in large areas of the country and its membership still a minority in the population as a whole, it was the best that the Dutch had, and it could at least be seen with some truth as the church of the governing élites everywhere in the Republic, particularly after the purges of 1618. This is the Dutch version of the European phenomenon of confessionalisation: a narrower definition of reformed orthodoxy together with a closer identification of the state with the Reformed Church. However, while the outcome preserved the privileges of the Church and ensured a monopoly on political office for its members, it left the religious diversity of the Republic intact. The brief, though fierce, persecution of remonstrants was a temporary aberration arising from peculiarly threatening circumstances, and the forces working for toleration soon reasserted themselves.

Although the Republic seems to have been as susceptible as the rest of Europe to belief in magic and witchcraft, it very largely escaped the panic witch hunts of the time and, indeed, ended routine prosecution of witches well before the rest of Europe.[19] As in other matters, however, there were considerable differences between the provinces and some areas did experience the witch craze, at least briefly. In general it seems to be the case that the economically and socially most advanced provinces were least affected by the witch craze and ended prosecutions earliest, while the regions with a more traditional socio-economic structure were more susceptible. It must be stressed, however, that what is concerned here is variation in the willingness of judicial authorities to try and condemn accused witches, not the intensity of belief in, or the frequency of accusation, of witchcraft. Both routine prosecutions for witchcraft and the witch crazes proper relied on the interplay of popular beliefs and accusations and a judicial system willing to take them seriously. In the Republic, in Holland and Zeeland first, and in the other provinces not long after, it was the scepticism of the courts which brought the trials to a halt, not the ending of belief in the reality of witchcraft in the population at large. It may well be, however, that while continuing in a general sense to believe in witchcraft, Dutch people were beginning to feel less immediately threatened by it, at least in the more economically developed regions.

That the Republic was less plagued by the witch hunt than most of the rest of Europe[20] was a triumph for practice rather than theory. There were sceptical voices raised in and around the Netherlands in the sixteenth century, and these became louder and more influential in the seventeenth, but they only slowly made inroads into traditional beliefs among the educated and had little impact on the population at large. It is clear that belief in magic in general and various forms of witchcraft in particular continued at the popular level throughout the seventeenth century and beyond.[21]

Fantasies about the sabbat seem to have been weak or absent altogether, but belief in *maleficia* – harm done by magical means – remained an integral part of the life of country people in particular. The church may have ceased to pursue witches through its disciplinary system, but it continued to regard belief in witches and the active intervention of the devil into everyday life as necessary to faith. Even in the last decades of the seventeenth century challenging this particular part of traditional beliefs could create a storm of passionate opposition from ministers of the Reformed Church, as Balthasar Bekker found.[22]

It seems clear that the rapid growth of the maritime provinces undermined the economic and social basis of the belief system of which witchcraft was a part, through urbanisation, the triumph of the market and greater prosperity. However, only towards the end of the century – in the period of the pre-Enlightenment – was a successful conceptual challenge mounted against the traditional magical universe; before this point, the educated, and particularly those involved in the law and medicine, had become sceptical about witchcraft trials but not about witchcraft: they doubted whether those actually accused of the crime were witches, and they were unhappy about the judicial irregularities which seemed necessary to bring successful prosecutions in such cases, but in the main they did not deny the reality of witchcraft. By the end of the century, the degree of political support that Bekker received suggests that a more general scepticism was gaining ground, and the later Enlightenment repudiation of the magical universe was already clearly foreshadowed in these years. Yet such issues remained highly sensitive and the old system of beliefs was far from dead even at the end of the century.

The religious toleration which marked the Republic off from the rest of Europe in this century, however grudging and partial it may have been, was only made possible by the emergence of new social and political priorities. As long as religious purity remained of prime importance, and as long as it was believed that there was only one religious truth, toleration would be a sin not a virtue – as indeed many outraged contemporary comments on the situation in the Republic show. So the priority given by the authorities to such values as order and prosperity suggests at least the beginnings of a secularised society within the Dutch state. Yet there are difficulties with this position: the regents who established these new priorities were not freethinkers but members of the Reformed Church and shared its values. Moreover, as we have seen, there were distinct limits to possible toleration: there could be no acknowledged or legal freedom of worship for catholics, and even some radical protestant beliefs remained beyond the pale – not to mention denial of the truth of christianity or of religion in general.[23]

The Republic was a christian society governed by a protestant state and shared much of the belief system which made religious persecution not just the norm but the ideal elsewhere in Europe. The actual religious divisions within Dutch society created the need for a theoretical justification of religious toleration, and to a large extent practice preceded theory. The peculiarities of the political system in the Republic meant that this pragmatic toleration developed at the grass roots level inspired by the need to preserve communal solidarity and protect local interests. Religion remained a powerful force in Dutch politics and society but after 1618 it was never again allowed to get out of hand and threaten the stability of the polity. Later disputes within the Reformed Church were contained with relative ease, despite their links with political antagonisms,[24] although the issues concerned seem from the theological point of view to be just as explosive. The religious diversity of the Republic came to be accepted as a fact of life, and a certain degree of toleration as inevitable; the theoretical justification of this practice may have been unimpressive, but relative religious peace in a divided society was no mean achievement for the time.

5

A BOURGEOIS SOCIETY?

It is generally accepted that the northern provinces of the Netherlands underwent an economic transformation which began sometime in the late fifteenth or early sixteenth century and took off about a century later. This process was most marked in the maritime provinces, with Holland – of course – in the lead, but even the land provinces were also profoundly affected by the changes in the country as a whole. That economic developments on this scale inevitably had significant social consequences is not in dispute; what historians are not agreed on is the nature of the society which was created by these developments. By the late seventeenth century it seems clear that the first completely capitalist economy in history had emerged in the Republic but, oddly enough, there seems to be a near-consensus among historians that what would seem to be the indispensable social corollary of capitalism – the bourgeoisie – did not and indeed could not exist at this time in any meaningful sense.[1] This debate aside, the question still remains whether the economic changes were far-reaching enough to produce new social formations and, if so, whether such a transformation was limited to the maritime provinces. It is clear that different regions of the Republic were affected in very different ways by the economic developments of the sixteenth and seventeenth centuries, and it may well be that some social groups were more profoundly affected than others, but whether a new type of society emerged is more difficult to determine.

On the other hand, it is possible to argue that the growth in the economy involved a change in scale rather than in type. From this point of view, the urban economy of the late middle ages was already thoroughly commercial and its subsequent growth was essentially an expansion in size and scope which left the economic and social structure more or less unchanged. Of course, changes of scale must at some point lead to change of type, and by 1700 both individual towns and the economic system within which they operated had changed enormously. Moreover, if the highly developed Dutch economy of the late seventeenth century was essentially only the late medieval urban economy writ large, then the implication seems to be that something like a capitalist economy was already present in essence in the towns of the Netherlands before the spectacular growth of the sixteenth and seventeenth centuries. If this was the case then a bourgeoisie too – far from being unthinkable in the early modern period – must have existed in some sense at this earlier time as well, a thought which is heretical but not perhaps inherently absurd.

Many historians find the term bourgeoisie too reminiscent of Marxist dogmatics to be used with any equanimity, and have sought more neutral terms. The Dutch terms *burger* and *burgerij* have the advantage that they are rooted in the period itself, but they have taken on a considerable emotive loading since that time, and have became as much a part of the language of social polemic as the term bourgeoisie itself. A burgher was a citizen with specific rights (as opposed to a mere inhabitant) and in general belonged to the solid middling groups in urban society, but did the burghers in the towns of the northern Netherlands at the beginning of the sixteenth century constitute quite the same social formation as their namesakes in the middle of the seventeenth century? Again the question is whether the increased size both absolutely – and, probably, relatively – of this group necessarily involved a change in type. In other words, were the middling classes of the Holland towns in the seventeenth century an expanded version of the late medieval *burgerij* or a new social class? The new society of the seventeenth-century towns undoubtedly already existed at least in embryo at the beginning of the great boom, but in the northern Netherlands – in contrast to the great towns of Flanders and Brabant – the towns at that time were relatively small. Here the social as well as economic changes in the course of the sixteenth and seventeenth centuries were considerable, and in Holland massive. Even if the social structure of the towns of Holland remained more or less the same – which can be doubted – the change of scale alone, especially in relation to the rest of society, suggests that a new form of society had appeared.

The term bourgeoisie implies the emergence of a new class while burger is redolent of the old society of orders, and there were elements of both in the middling groups in Dutch urban society in the seventeenth century. Perhaps in the end the answer can only be cultural: sceptics claim that a class cannot exist without class-consciousness; if so, it becomes a question of how the middling groups in Dutch society saw themselves and how they perceived the world in which they lived.

Dutch economic development was most obviously marked by rapid growth of the towns and a high degree of urbanisation, but the transformation of the countryside was just as important and perhaps even more far-reaching.[2] In brief, in the course of the sixteenth and early seventeenth centuries the rural sector became thoroughly integrated into the booming market economy with consequent radical changes in social relations in the countryside. These developments would seem to have been restricted to the maritime provinces – Holland, Zeeland, parts of Friesland and Groningen – while the eastern and inland areas, although powerfully affected by this dynamic agrarian modernisation, responded in rather different ways and with distinctly different social consequences. Not least of the problems facing the land provinces was that they found themselves in competition with the highly commercialised agriculture of the maritime region. In Holland, the developments of the early sixteenth century saw the beginning of the decisive transformation of agriculture to specialised production for the market. The farmers benefited from the opportunities offered by the province's expanding commercial economy, but more immediately they were able to take advantage of the demand coming from the growing towns – about half the population of Holland was already living in towns by the middle of the sixteenth century, so Holland's farmers had a peculiarly favourable local market even at this early stage of the economic transformation. In return, the rural sector became a market for Baltic grain and a wide range of services provided by the towns. In this way, the rural sector became an integral part of the development of a fully commercial economy from the end of the middle ages onwards. The drainage problems at this time[3] which were particularly acute in North Holland also stimulated economic diversification in the countryside, especially the development of craft production and involvement in trade and fishing. It is worth remembering that De Rijp, a large village in the centre of North Holland, was heavily involved in the herring fisheries by the late sixteenth century. It is also a reminder that while water may have been a major problem for the Dutch, it also offered significant opportunities: the many rivers and canals provided a transport system which could reach all parts of Holland.

By the middle of the seventeenth century, Holland's rural sector was both market-oriented and highly specialised, producing dairy products, meat and other goods for both a local and an international market, and in turn becoming customers for the foods and other products which they could no longer provide for themselves. A similar development took place in the rest of the maritime region of the Republic, certainly in Zeeland and the coastal areas of Friesland. The land provinces, however, were another matter: they did not have the same problems with water as Holland, were much more dependent on agriculture, but were powerfully affected by the growth of a specialised and highly efficient agriculture so close to them. By the seventeenth century the pull of the Holland market, and particularly the enormous demand from Amsterdam, seems to have dominated the rural economy of these provinces. The market opportunities available to the producers in the land provinces were balanced by the difficulties of competing with the highly developed agriculture of Holland itself. One consequence was greater caution on the part of the farmers: in Drenthe, for example, farmers diversified not to maximise profits but to minimise the danger of failure – in the circumstances perhaps a rational economic response.[4]

The increased market orientation and specialisation of the rural economy involved far-reaching structural changes. In Holland there was a steady increase in the size of farms, and in the proportion of agricultural land held by larger farms. The smaller peasant holdings declined in number and importance, and indeed the peasant in the conventional sense had practically disappeared from Holland by the end of the seventeenth century. The maritime region was increasingly dominated by large-scale capitalist farmers, producing for the market, and hiring labour and specialised services when needed. This development in turn stimulated the growth of a service sector in the country-side, providing artisan, transport and other services. The intensity of commercial penetration meant that there was a large-scale demand for water transport, in particular in the rural areas. Indeed, the opportunity provided for cheap transport of goods by rivers, lakes and canals in the maritime region was important in making the intensification of trading contacts possible. By the later seventeenth century, there was no sharp and clear-cut distinction between town and countryside in Holland. Instead a hierarchy of towns and villages can be traced according to the range of services and facilities they were able to provide; the larger towns, naturally, had most to offer, but the smaller towns and larger villages still had a quite impressive range of services, and there was a smooth gradation from large town to small village with no sharp breaks on the way.[5] In addition to the obvious economic services – and, of course, churches and meeting places to serve the various religious needs of the local community – many of the larger villages also had a doctor or surgeon, a notary or lawyer, and even a hospital or orphanage. Some villages grew to the size of small towns: Graft reached a population of 3000 or over in the seventeenth century, and the nearby De Rijp was probably even larger. A special case is the agglomeration of industrial villages in the *Zaanstreek* which became the centre of shipbuilding, sawmilling, and associated industries. In the course of the seventeenth century the population of this area grew to over 20 000, and it must be regarded as a town as far as its economic function is concerned, even though it remained administratively and formally just a collection of villages. The availability of a wide range of goods and services throughout the Holland countryside – and the same can be said to a greater or lesser degree for the maritime region as a whole – is an illustration of the growing economic and social diversification of the rural sector. The changes in social structure in the countryside are among the most spectacular consequences of the great economic boom.

As far as rural society is concerned, two main directions of change can be discerned: on the one hand a process of polarisation between capitalist farmer and hired labour; and on the other hand the growth in the number of people involved in the service sector, producing a species of rural middle class. The concentration of land into large commercial enterprises, hiring labour and services when needed, brought capitalist relations of production to the farming community. It also effectively squeezed out the smallholder, a process facilitated by the decline of river and lake fisheries as a result of the drainage schemes. Indeed, it has been suggested that this structural change led to the disappearance from Holland of cheap labour for the textile industry by the later seventeenth century, that is peasant smallholders who could support their families in part from their plots and thus could work for manufacturers for less than a living wage. This stratum of the rural population had practically disappeared in Holland and manufacturers had to move to areas such as Twenthe (in Overijssel) and North Brabant to find a cheap rural workforce.[6] A contrasting development was the growth in the number of skilled artisans, shopkeepers and traders, boatmen and shippers, notaries and teachers in the countryside. A significant proportion of the rural population was also dependent, to some extent at least, on employment in the fishing industry and the merchant fleet. It should also be remembered that the booming towns provided an outlet for any surplus population in the rural areas, thus facilitating change and minimising its social cost. Although such economic and social diversity in the countryside can already be seen at the beginning of the sixteenth century, the rural sector had been transformed into a recognisably modern society a century and a half later.

Such radical changes were confined to the maritime region, and the picture in the land provinces was very different. Here the old social structures, though put under considerable strain, survived more or less intact. The pace of demographic growth was much less severe in these areas, and the power of the nobles and other landowners considerably greater than in Holland. Although generalisation on this subject is even more fraught with difficulties than usual, it can be suggested that there was a trend towards a deterioration of the conditions of the dependent peasantry, and that freeholders continued to suffer from the economic and political dominance of the nobility and other rural notables. These areas were particularly hard hit by the general stagnation of prices that affected the rural economy in the later seventeenth century – the first major sign of the downturn of the Dutch economy.

The changes which took place in the Dutch countryside were of profound importance for the development of the economy as a whole, but the growth and importance of the towns was the most obvious way in which the Republic differed from the greater part of the rest of Europe. It was not just the number and size of the towns but the high proportion of the total population that lived in them: by the mid seventeenth century the level of urbanisation had reached levels which were equalled in the rest of Europe only after industrialisation. Even for the northern Netherlands as a whole the figures are impressive: already in the early sixteenth century urbanisation had reached a little over 30 per cent, and by about 1675 this had risen to 45 per cent. For the province of Holland, however, the best available statistics suggest that a decisive break had taken place with the past by the middle of the seventeenth century. Here almost 45 per cent of the population already lived in towns by c.1525, and this proportion probably approached 50 per cent by the middle of that century; by about 1675 the proportion had risen to over 60 per cent.[7] Here, and to a lesser degree in the maritime region as a whole, a recognisably modern residential and work pattern had emerged, and it was to be 150 – or more – years before this level was equalled by the industrialising England of the early nineteenth century. In Holland the towns grew rapidly and the degree of urbanisation increased up to the last quarter of the seventeenth century but, within this general pattern, there were important variations for individual towns. Growth appears to have been general in the sixteenth century, speeding up noticeably from the 1580s onwards after the difficulties during the earlier years of the Revolt. This phase of more or less uniform urban expansion, however, only lasted till the 1620s, after which many of the smaller towns of the province began to experience difficulties, and growth continued at the same pace only in the larger towns, especially Amsterdam, Leiden, Rotterdam, and the administrative centre, The Hague. Enkhuizen had a particularly spectacular growth up to about 1620 but then ran into serious difficulties, and the other major trading centre in the Northern Quarter of Holland, Hoorn, also encountered insurmountable economic problems by the middle of the century. After about 1675 even the larger towns hit the buffers and overall growth ceased. The subsequent depression affected the smaller towns most severely: the bigger centres in the main experienced stagnation but only minor falls in their population. The chief exceptions to this rule were Leiden and Haarlem, which were very heavily dependent on a textile industry which was in precipitous decline by the end of the century. Haarlem's decline possibly set in as early as the 1640s while Leiden seems to have continued to expand until the 1670s, but in both cases the economic malaise led to a demographic decline which assumed major proportions in the following century.

This growth in the size of the towns was accompanied by what might be called an urbanisation of the smaller towns and villages of the province, as the whole of Holland was brought into the commercial system based in the towns. It is also significant that this urban growth was fairly evenly spread, at least up to the 1620s. Amsterdam became the biggest town by the census of 1622 and easily maintained this lead for the rest of the century. By about 1680 its population was probably about 200 000, which was a quarter of the total for Holland as a whole, and nearly three times the size of its nearest rival, but it never had the sort of preponderance that London had in contemporary England. At this time, the population of Leiden was c.65 000, Rotterdam c.45 000, and Haarlem c.37 000, while Delft and Dordrecht each had 20 000–25 000 inhabitants. Below these were another four towns with over

10 000 inhabitants and a further three over 5000. Urban growth and prosperity marked the whole province, though the level of urbanisation was noticeably higher in South Holland than in the Northern Quarter. In addition some places outside the towns acquired distinctly urban characteristics, as we have seen, and many of the larger villages became active trade centres, while those of the *Zaanstreek* became collectively the centre of Dutch shipbuilding and associated manufactures. The towns used their local political clout – and the 18 voting-towns their control of the States of Holland – to inhibit rural manufactures that might compete directly with their own products,[8] but their need to integrate the countryside into their commercial systems stimulated the development of a dense trading and transport system throughout the province. One of the most characteristic elements of Holland's economic success in the late sixteenth and early seventeenth centuries was its ubiquity: though some towns fared better than others, all shared in the boom to some extent, and the advantages spread to the smaller towns and villages as well. Just as the rural sector was firmly integrated into the province's powerful commercial economy, so all settlements from the greatest to the smallest were united by a system of mutually beneficial economic and trading links. However, it is equally true that one of the first indications that something was going fundamentally wrong with Holland's economy was the appearance of wide disparities in economic experience. Well before the middle of the seventeenth century both the most successful trading centres of North Holland, Enkhuizen and Hoorn, began to suffer from the competition of Amsterdam's powerful economy, among other problems, and they moved into a period of stagnation followed by decline. By the end of the century, it had become clear that trade was increasingly becoming concentrated on a few towns at the expense of the rest, and that the general decline in manufactures was hitting some towns – Leiden, Haarlem – much harder than others. The depression and the social dislocation it brought in its wake had already arrived in many parts of Holland well before the eighteenth century.

The social structure of the towns of Holland and of the maritime region in general, reflected the economic basis of their growth; with the notable exception of the administrative and court centre, The Hague, their economies were based on trade, shipping and manufactures. This led to an expansion of the middling groups in society to organise and manage trade, and to service the needs of merchants and traders at every level. At the bottom of this expanding middle class were the shopkeepers and small traders together with the artisans who ran their own businesses. The latter was a particularly broad category, ranging from the self-employed craftsman to producer-traders with considerable businesses and wealthy enough to be at least on the fringe of the urban élite. There was also a wide range of merchants from small and perhaps specialised family operations to enormous international enterprises such as those run by Trip and De Geer. The *Trippenhuis* in Amsterdam is a visual reminder of the social standing of these leading merchants – who were often, of course, a prominent part of the regent group of their towns as well. Trade and the innumerable business transactions it involved also needed the services, and stimulated the supply, of lawyers and notaries, and these were at the heart of a booming service sector in the expanding towns. Medical services, from university-trained doctors, through the craftsmen barber-surgeons, to self-taught midwives – not to mention a variegated collection of unofficial healers – grew with the wealth of the towns, even though there was little that they could do for the most serious problems facing the urban population, such as the plague. In the course of this period, the doctors were able to enhance their prestige and establish their effective control over the medical system, while the surgeons, coming together in guilds, were also able to improve their social status. Apothecaries too could do very well out of the new economic conditions, especially when they became involved in the trade in the expensive New World and Asian drugs and herbs that became such an important part of their stock in trade.

Such a complex economy also required a considerable supply of teaching and training services. Within a few years of the Revolt from Spain, Holland had established a university at Leiden, and this example was followed in due course by the other provinces with greater or lesser success – Utrecht, Franeker (for Friesland), Groningen, Harderwijk (Gelderland). Some towns in Holland, such as Amsterdam and Rotterdam, had so-called Illustrious Schools which were institutions of higher education, but without degree-giving powers. All the major towns had their Latin Schools for the education of the social élite in true renaissance style, and there was a wide variety of vernacular schools teaching basic skills. In general the literacy rate was high in Holland, though less impressive for women than for men, and so it seems the great majority of the urban population had at least some contact with formal education. Literacy and numeracy were increasingly important skills in the market economy of both town and countryside in the maritime region. Whereas in the sixteenth century many of the middling groups in society were still signing with a mark, by the end of the seventeenth such a lack of basic literacy had become unusual above the level of the unskilled worker. Professors at the leading universities enjoyed considerable prestige, and the masters in the Latin Schools also benefited from the high status which continued to be attached to humanist learning. Below this level, teachers in basic education were less well rewarded either in income or in social status than those in the humanist mainstream, but were perhaps rather more competent and respectable than they have sometimes been depicted.

A rather different social profile developed in Leiden and Haarlem with their heavy dependence on wool and linen textiles. Elsewhere production was largely in the hands of artisan-traders employing a handful of apprentices and journeymen, here it was controlled by merchant entrepreneurs and the weavers and other skilled workers had been effectively reduced to the position of wage labourers. Social relations in these manufacturing centres were consequently much more polarised than in the trading towns, especially as cyclical depressions in the textile trade led to recurrent periods of severe unemployment. The workers of Leiden and Haarlem had a reputation for volatility which in retrospect looks suspiciously like class antagonism, though a number of historians insist that it did not exist at this time. The economic organisation of the textile industry was producing a sort of proto-proletariat, and this situation also had a noticeable physical impact on these towns. In most of the Holland towns rich, comfortable and poor lived more or less cheek by jowl: some wards were richer than others, but in the main the poor could be found in the side streets and alleys just round the corner from the well-off. In the textile towns, in contrast, areas of cheap housing were built to house the workers,[9] and so a physical as well as an economic divide was introduced, foreshadowing the conditions of the factory towns of a later period. Economic expansion also brought employment for large numbers of unskilled and semi-skilled workers almost everywhere in the province. The ports required large numbers of dockers and porters, as did transport in general, and these too could be a violent and unstable element in society – notably in Amsterdam which had the biggest concentration of such workers – but their numbers were proportionally much less important than those of the downgraded craftsmen in the textile towns.

The merchant fleet and the fishing industry were important sources of employment, not only in the port towns but also in the countryside.

Around 1680 it is estimated that the merchant fleet gave employment to 22 500 seamen, with another 8500 in the fleet of the VOC, and over 15 000 involved in (sea) fishing and whaling.[10] Of course, not all of the seamen came from Holland: many were from Zeeland and Friesland and, indeed, the demand for sailors was so great that it could only be met with the help of immigrants, especially from the coastal regions of north west Germany and Scandinavia. So short was the supply of sailors that the Dutch navy also had to resort to taking on foreigners, though to a much lesser extent than the army. It should be remembered that international conditions forced the Dutch to maintain a large army for the greater part of the century; numbers fluctuated considerably, but for long periods the state was employing over 50 000 and sometimes nearer 100 000 men in its land forces.[11] A high proportion of these, varying perhaps between 40 per cent and 60 per cent, were drawn from outside the Republic, but this still left the army as a very important employer, and even more so if foreign soldiers who settled permanently in the Republic are taken into consideration. In time of war, the navy also employed large numbers of men – it has been estimated that during the Third Anglo-Dutch War and the Nine Years War (1688–97) something in the region of 20 000–24 000 men were in naval service.[12]

An important characteristic of employment at sea, apart from its hardships and none too great rewards, was that it kept men away from their homes and families for long periods. This absence of men had inevitable consequences for the role of women in Dutch society; the wives of seamen not only had to fend for themselves and their children for much of the time, they also were often given powers-of-attorney to deal with their husbands' affairs during their absence at sea. The social effect of this peculiar role for sailor's wives was obviously greater in small communities with a heavy maritime orientation than in the larger ports with a more varied economic base, but the sheer numbers of men employed at sea meant that it was an important factor in the social life not only of the trading towns but of the rural areas of the maritime region as well. The fishing and merchant fleet was also an important indirect source of employment in shipbuilding and associated trades – the *Zaanstreek* was almost entirely based economically on shipbuilding and servicing the needs of shipping from sawmills and ropewalks to the baking of ships'-biscuits. Fishing likewise needed large numbers of people to handle the catch, from barrel-makers and packers to the bargees needed to transport it through and out of the country.

If a new form of society emerged in the most advanced areas of the Republic, this transformation did not spread to the rest of the country. Much of what has been said about the radical changes which had taken place in Dutch society by the end of the seventeenth century applies mainly if not only to the maritime region, and in particular Holland. It was here that the economic boom of the late sixteenth and early seventeenth centuries took place, and it was here that the consequent social transformation occurred. In the rest of the country, the population grew less explosively and the economic and social structure remained much more traditional. The land provinces also were much more directly affected by the war with Spain than Holland: up to the middle of the seventeenth century the economy of the whole region was constantly disturbed by the movement of troops, sieges, and the levying of contributions by the rival armies. Such circumstances made these provinces even less able to defend themselves successfully against the economic competition of the maritime region. The frontier between the two regions ran through some of the provinces and was not always clear; the economic success of Holland was shared to some extent at least by Zeeland, the coastal areas of Friesland, together with parts of Groningen and Utrecht, while the remaining parts of these latter provinces together with Overijssel, Gelderland and North Brabant comprised the relatively backward section of the country. This poorer region covered over half the Republic's geographical area, though the greater demographic growth of the maritime region meant that it encompassed less than half of the total population by the middle of the seventeenth century. For a large part of the Republic the seventeenth century was, economically at least, far from being a Golden Century.

In the rural sector, modernisation on the pattern set by Holland was restricted to the maritime region, but the land provinces nevertheless experienced considerable changes, not least under the powerful pressure of the Holland market. Gelderland and Overijssel, for example, experienced much slower demographic growth, and much of this increase seems not to have been absorbed in booming towns but to have remained on the land and increased the number of peasants with access to only very small plots of land. Drenthe similarly became increasingly dependent on serving the Amsterdam market, but the result was not highly specialised commercial farming as in Holland, but mixed farming on properties which remained relatively small. In general agriculture in these areas was drawn steadily into the thrall of the market but here, in contrast to the profitable large-scale commercial farming of Holland, it could only compete by lowering the rewards and living standards of smallholders and workers on the land. The continued social domination of the region as a whole by nobles and local notables further weakened the situation for the middle-sized and small farmers. It was only in the eighteenth century that the freeholders of Gelderland and Overijssel began to agitate to break out of their political impotence, and even then they made little impact before the end of the Republic. The economic malaise of this region made it to a degree a colonial region of the Holland economy, and one way in which this showed was in the stream of poor migrants leaving the land provinces to seek employment in the towns of the dominant province, and especially in Amsterdam. Some of this migration was temporary, at least in intent: young men and women hoping to be able to earn enough to make a sound start on married life in their native villages, but for many it was permanent, not least because of the high death rate in the towns they were going to. The needs of the Holland economy also stimulated other changes in the region: textile manufacturers in search of cheap labour settled on Twente and North Brabant, areas with large numbers of smallholding peasants available to work for the new industries at less than subsistence rates. These notoriously poverty-stricken areas were able eventually to compete successfully with the textile towns of Holland because the social structure in the countryside here had not modernised in the way it had in the maritime region. However, although these new industries brought employment to these areas, they exploited the poverty of the region rather than alleviating it.

The contrast with the maritime region was even more obvious in the urban sector. The towns of the land provinces grew much more slowly than those of Holland, and the degree of urbanisation was much lower than in the maritime region. The proportion of the population living in towns in the land provinces grew only marginally up to the middle of the seventeenth century, and in size their towns were by this time overshadowed by their counterparts in Holland. The leading towns of the region in particular were badly hit by competition from Holland. Deventer, Kampen and Zwolle as members of the Hansa had had an important role in extra-regional trade in the later middle ages, but from the sixteenth century onwards found their long-distance trade increasingly undermined by the seaborne commerce of Holland, and particularly by Amsterdam's direct trade with the Baltic and north Germany. Their ability to compete with these formidable rivals was undermined by the continuous warfare of the late sixteenth and early seventeenth centuries which disturbed the inland routes to neighbouring regions of Germany which were so important to them. In consequence these IJssel towns lost much of their international trade and were reduced almost to the position of local market towns.

The social structure of the towns of the region also remained much more traditional: manufactures remained on a relatively small scale, there was little opportunity for the development of major mercantile enterprises, and the local nobility kept much of their social and political influence. In short, urban life here changed relatively little in structure during a period when what town life meant was being dramatically transformed in nearby Holland. Much the same can be said for the society of the land provinces in general: despite the economic stresses of the period the social structure remained more or less intact. The relatively greater dependence of the region on agriculture, however, brought particular problems after the onset of the depression in agricultural rents and prices which set in in the second half of the seventeenth century. The incomes of landlords as well as farmers and smallholders were hit severely in the long run – not helped by tax increases to bolster up ever more shaky provincial and state finances – but the region as a whole because of its more traditional economic structure was perhaps not as vulnerable to the changing economic climate as the Holland towns. In the eighteenth century, the economic balance began to swing in favour of the rural sector, especially after agricultural prices began to pick up in the second half of the century, and away from the towns of Holland which – with the exception of Amsterdam, Rotterdam and a few others – were in full demographic and economic decline. The boom may have been hardly noticeable in the land provinces, but the bust was probably less painful.

Half the population, more or less, of the Republic was female and around half of these were adult women. This statement may seem so obvious as to be redundant, but it reminds us that women were not a minority, oppressed or otherwise, and have to be treated as an integral part of contemporary society, as in an important sense they no more have a separate history than do men. However, it is still difficult to integrate women fully into conventional history – even social history – and so, however undesirable in principle, it still seems useful to give at least a brief consideration to the peculiar experience of women in the Golden Century. Unfortunately, in the present state of research there is still much that is unclear particularly with regard to the economic role and activities of women in the rapidly changing society of the period. Considerable light has, however, been thrown on certain areas, and it is also possible to suggest at least some of the ways the position and possibilities for women were affected both by the economic and social transformation of the maritime region and by the less dynamic conditions in the rest of the Republic.[13] One thing is clear however: this was not a society which could afford to keep its women in idleness or confined to a purely domestic role. At every level of society, except for the nobility and the most wealthy sections of the bourgeoisie, women's work was necessary for the family's economic survival. However, there is some evidence to suggest that in the process of economic modernisation women were becoming increasingly marginalised. The commercial transformation of the rural sector in Holland in particular would seem to have led to roles which had formerly belonged to women being usurped by men as they became economically more important.

Women provided the backbone of domestic service, and the demand for servants remained high particularly in the growing towns where some help was regarded as indispensable in all but the poorest of homes, and where an impressive number of servants was equally necessary to the prestige of richer households. A period of domestic service was a normal part of a woman's lifecycle in much of Europe at this time, and was often the most obvious way to scrape together enough money or goods to be able to marry.[14] The high and rising demand for servants in the towns of Holland led to the development of a pattern of both internal and longer distance migration. Many of the servants in the towns of Holland were drawn from the country areas of the province, but this supply could not fill all the available posts and young women from the other provinces were drawn to Holland. Amsterdam in particular, with its enormous demand for domestice service of all sorts began to recruit its female servants from much further afield. In the course of the seventeenth century there developed a steady stream of immigrant servants travelling to Amsterdam via the Zuider Zee ports from neighbouring areas of Germany, and a similar link developed by sea from coastal areas of Norway. Many of these, perhaps most, intended to return home to marry and settle when they had earned enough money, but many stayed either from choice or necessity.

Young servant girls a long way from home were vulnerable to sexual exploitation by male fellow servants, and more especially by the males of the family employing them, and the disaster of an unwanted pregnancy was a common professional hazard. Midwives attending unmarried mothers were instructed to pressure them into revealing the name of the father, so that he could legally be coerced into supporting the child, but this still left the immigrant servant girl with her hopes of a respectable marriage shattered. Whether by this route or through other misfortunes, a significant proportion of the prostitutes who proliferated in the towns, notably in the ports of Holland, came from elsewhere and often from outside the Republic. In this part of the service sector at least the contribution of women was indispensable (there is no evidence for homosexual male prostitution on any regular basis), and the organisation of the business seems also to have been largely in female hands.[15]

What the consequences for women in general were of the far-reaching economic changes in the maritime region in the course of the late sixteenth and early seventeenth centuries is as yet difficult to assess, and in any case will almost certainly prove to be ambivalent. In the towns, the growing size of the upper bourgeoisie increased the number, and perhaps the proportion, of women with a purely domestic role, foreshadowing to some extent the pattern of middle-class respectability in nineteenth-century industrial society. The triumph of large-scale commercial farming in the Holland countryside may also have reduced the prominence of women's economic activities. As dairying, for example, moved from being only a part of a farm's activities and largely in the women's domain to constituting the main business of a primarily market-oriented rural industry, it came under male control, though still retaining a female workforce in the dairies. In the less developed agriculture of the land provinces, in contrast, the small-scale production of butter and cheese remained women's business. (It also continued to be one of the most important foci of witchcraft suspicions and accusations in these regions[16] – in this highly personal production system the failure of butter to churn aroused fears and suspicions that seem largely to have disappeared from the commercialised dairy-farming of Holland.) Similarly, there is some evidence to suggest that the shortage of labour in the long demographic depression after the Black Death allowed at least some women into skilled occupations, but they were squeezed out again during the prolonged phase of demographic expansion stretching from the late fifteenth to around the middle of the seventeenth century.[17] On the other hand the continued importance of artisan production in the manufacturing sector meant that the contribution of wives remained crucial to the successful running of these innumerable small businesses. Guild regulations often allowed a widow to carry on the family business after her husband's death, at least for a while; and one of the routes for an ambitious journeyman to become an independent master was to marry a master's widow – which demonstrates the status and at least latent social power of the wife in this section of society.

Whether in the towns or in the countryside women and girls worked, and were expected to work; it has been calculated that families in the unskilled and semi-skilled level of society could not survive without the economic contribution of women – and indeed of children as well.[18] Although in the main women were paid less than men,[19] they never-theless played an important role throughout the economy. Women were particularly prominent in small-scale retailing, running market stalls and small shops: in this area the presence and indeed the voices of women dominated the scene. However, their general exclusion from training or apprenticeships for skilled crafts meant that they were employed in unskilled or semi-skilled work, or rather in occupations where the relevant skills were not recognised formally and certainly not in the form of high pay. Women's role as carers and healers was largely taken for granted as part of their household tasks, and even when a degree of recognition was given to the particular expertise and experi-ence of some women this could be fragile. Midwives enjoyed some status in the sixteenth century, and most towns had municipal midwives with quite wide responsibilities but, with the increasing professionalisa-tion of health care in the course of the seventeenth century, they were progressively brought under the control of male doctors and surgeons, and their status plummeted. Even in those crafts where the physical differences between male and female were least relevant, such as paint-ing, very few women were in fact able to break through the barriers erected by conventional ideas as to what women should, and prejudices about what they could, do. It is notable that among the large numbers of professional painters produced in the Golden Age only a handful were women.

The nobility do not figure prominently in conventional accounts of the Dutch Republic, but they were there.[20] Indeed, one of the problems in assessing the nature of Dutch society at this time is understanding to what extent and why the nobles were able to maintain their political and social importance despite the rapid social and economic change which might have been expected to undermine their position. Even in Holland, it has recently been argued, the nobility retained much more political power and social influence than used to be thought[21] and, though the point might be a little overstated, it does seem to be true that there was no direct attack on the principle of the superior status of nobles. In the land provinces, the much slower rate of change and relative structural stability of society allowed the nobility to retain a great part of its social as well as political dominance.

In Gelderland, Overijssel and Utrecht the nobility shared political power with the towns, but were in many ways the dominant partners. They were also an increasingly closed group: whereas a certain amount of social mobility was still possible in the sixteenth century, with new families able to enter the nobility, by the later part of the succeeding century the nobles had successfully closed their ranks. A seat on the noble delegation to the provincial estates (ridderschap) of these provinces and access to the other judical and political privileges of the nobility became restricted to a sharply defined set of established families. This kept power and the profits of office in the hands of a few privileged families, but exposed the group as a whole to demographic erosion. By the beginning of the eighteenth century numbers had fallen dramatically, which was good news for the survivors but augured badly for the survival of the nobility as a whole.

In Friesland and Groningen the position was rather more complex; these areas had been barely touched by the feudal system and the nature of the local nobility was in consequence less clear and its powers less firmly established than in the central land provinces. In Friesland, a new oligarchy established itself in the seventeenth century, particularly through the manipulation of its peculiar political system in the countryside, but this was a mixture of the old nobility with town regents and was thus markedly different from the traditional nobility of the land provinces. In Groningen the country areas (Ommelanden) were dominated by an emergent oligarchy of landowners with noble pretensions, who were also successful in closing themselves off from outsiders in the course of the century. In both cases the nobility as a whole was vulnerable demographically, and in Friesland was visibly dying out by the eighteenth century. In all these provinces, the nobility combined high social status with extensive political privileges and power. The nobles possessed considerable amounts of land and owned substantial country houses – indeed in some provinces (Utrecht, Overijssel, Drenthe) ownership of designated castles or landed property was a prerequisite for membership of the *ridderschap* – but the strength of their position came to a great extent from their ability to manipulate the political system and to milk the profits of office. The countryside of Gelderland was dominated by a handful of nobles, the *landjonkers*, who were able to use the control of the judical and tax systems to their own considerable advantage. Ownership of manors or lordships (*heerlijkheden*) was also a typical mark of nobility but, while they may have enhanced the local influence of nobles, their contribution to noble finances seems to have been relatively small. In any case, by the later seventeenth century many *heerlijkheden* throughout the country had come into the hands of urban regents or other non-nobles, blurring to some extent the distinction between nobles and the urban élite. In Holland, the nobles were much less powerful in the states of the province though, as the system required noble representation on all important commissions and committees of the States, their situation was not without its possibilities. Economically, also, they were as a body a negligible force, even in the countryside as most land in Holland was in the hands of non-nobles. Also, here as elsewhere, the nobility was declining; indeed, by the end of the century it was clearly on its way to extinction. The fundamental problem was that there were no new creations during the Republican period to make up for demographic failures. After the repudiation of Philip II there was no ruler to create new nobles and, although the sovereign claims of the provincial states might have enabled them to carry out ennoblements, they never did so, and foreign creations were not fully recognised. Thus even in those provinces where the nobles enjoyed high status and great political power their numbers were declining in the course of the seventeenth century, and had fallen to critical levels before the end of the next century. The Dutch nobility was only saved by wholesale creations under the newly established monarchy in the nineteenth century. So the nobility had a much higher social profile than may have been expected in a bourgeois state. Moreover, it has been argued that the regents, far from being the representatives of bourgeois aspirations, were themselves subject to a far-reaching degree of aristocratisation. Admittedly, this is largely based on eighteenth-century evidence and largely anecdotal at that, but the process is said to have been well on the way by the end of the seventeenth century. Briefly, the argument is that the regents, even or particularly in Holland, were becoming a separate urban aristocracy, distinct in political power, economic interests, ideology, and lifestyle, from the rest of the urban middle classes. It is pointed out that many of them bought country estates, purchased *heerlijkheden* to give themselves quasi-noble titles, and moved away from any active involvement in trade or manufactures. However, even in the eighteenth century it is difficult to distinguish the lifestyle of the regents from that of the upper reaches of the urban middle classes. The latter, for example, also bought country retreats: these were modest affairs but then so were those of the great majority of the regents. The palatial mansions along the Vecht built by the richest of the regents of Amsterdam were quite untypical of the regent *buiten* even in the eighteenth century. The leading regent families of the larger towns are only a small part of the picture. Even in Holland there were great differences between the Amsterdam regents and those of the smaller towns, who were much less wealthy and lived in a distinctly more modest manner, and the regents in the rest of the Republic were even less aristocratic figures. On the available evidence it must be concluded that, until the end of the seventeenth century at least, the regents shared the attitudes and way of life of the upper bourgeoisie of their towns and in general can be regarded as representing their interests in broad terms.

The transformation of both urban and rural economies in the course of the late sixteenth and seventeenth centuries in the maritime region as a whole produced a society with a markedly modern social profile. The dominance of the market created a farming sector divided between capitalist farmers and hired labour backed up by a large and varied service sector; in the towns the great trading and manufacturing boom stimulated the growth of the small producers, shopkeepers and traders, and again a significant service sector, as well as the more spectacular large-scale merchants and manufacturers. Underneath were the sailors, fishermen, dockers and the like to provide an incipient proletariat. However, this radical change was restricted to the maritime region and was perhaps only complete in Holland; the rest of the Republic remained much more traditional both economically and socially. If a truly bourgeois society arose in the Republic, it was largely confined to Holland, affected the maritime region to some extent, but had only a very limited impact on the rest – which comprised, it should be remembered, at least half the territory of the Republic.

A new form of society did emerge in the Netherlands, but only in part of it, and in Europe as a whole it was only a very small part of a culture dominated by very different standards than those that can be seen as appropriate to capitalism. In these circumstances it is hardly surprising that a full bourgeois class consciousness is more than a little elusive. There was a bourgeoisie in the Republic, but it lacked a mature class consciousness. The cultural equivalent of the newly established bourgeois society was emerging in the seventeenth century also, but a confident and self-conscious assertion of middle-class values was far to seek.

6

A DIVIDED CULTURE

The Dutch have long regarded the seventeenth century as their Golden Century, and it is perhaps the cultural achievements of the period which have become its defining characteristic for later generations. After the resonance of economic domination, great power status, and colonial expansion had faded, the achievements of Dutch artists, writers and thinkers came to be seen as what made the period great; already by the late nineteenth century it had become the land of Rembrandt, rather than of De Witt, or even of the merchant.[1] Alongside the flowering of 'high' culture, there was also a broader cultural change, which has received less attention but was perhaps more profound, reflecting the transformation of Dutch society at the time. In neither case, however, was there a simple correlation between social and cultural change, and the persistence of traditional forms and perceptions was greater than than might have been expected.

The foundation of the new state was accompanied by the rapid creation of a Dutch cultural identity, particularly through the cultivation of traditional intellectual disciplines on more or less conventional lines. By the early seventeenth century, the Republic had become perhaps the most important centre for classical studies in Europe, building on the foundation of the flourishing humanism of the Netherlands in the previous century. This process was stimulated by the foundation of new universities, starting with Leiden in Holland in 1576. Although the initial purpose of these new institutions was primarily the training of ministers for the embryonic protestant church, they also provided employment for many of the leading humanists and a focus for their teaching and writings. In addition to the prestige which this pre-eminence in classical studies conferred on the European

129

stage, these new universities established a sound reputation in the traditional core disciplines of theology, law and medicine, with the latter rapidly gaining esteem for innovative teaching methods.

A conscious effort was also made to produce a literature in Dutch which would bear comparison to that in the leading vernaculars in Europe, based on the example of the classics and written according to the canons of literary excellence established during the renaissance. The aim was not to create a body of work that was distinctively Dutch, but to produce a Dutch literature that was respectable in the eyes of the rest of Europe. Such developments reflected the need of an emerging country to find a cultural expression for its new condition, as much to reinforce a rather uncertain sense of identity as to impress the outside world. However, the new identity while it had to be distinctive could not afford to be too different from the European norm, because this was the standard by which cultural achievements were judged. Moreover, the educated élite in the Republic were as committed to these common European values as were their counterparts elsewhere: from this perspective too distinctive a culture would be necessarily inferior.

On the other hand, the economic and social changes of this time were also beginning to transform Dutch culture. In particular, the power of market forces began to have an impact on both cultural forms and their content. The most obvious example of this is the way in which the nature of the market for art influenced the development of Dutch painting in the seventeenth century: much of what was new in the production of the Dutch School can be attributed to the nature of the demand.[2] There are less obvious, but no less important, links to be drawn between the changes in Dutch society and new modes of perception informing political thinking, philosophy and theology in this period, and – although this matter is as yet hardly explored – scientific developments have also to be understood in this context. Certainly, as the impact of economic and social forces was greater in some areas than in others, so some regions of the Republic were distinctly more conservative in cultural terms than the more developed areas.

The province of Holland was the centre of cultural change and innovation: here was the greatest prosperity and here also the most far-reaching changes in society took place. In comparison, the rest of the Republic appears rather conservative, though this perception may disguise the degree to which underlying structures were changing there as well. On the other hand, the strength of inherited ideas and perceptions should not be underestimated: from the proper place of

religion and the church in society to the standards of literary judgement, traditional ideas remained powerful. In culture as elsewhere, the
Republic saw a struggle between old and new, with the victory of the
latter far from self-evident or pre-ordained.

The seventeenth century was undoubtedly the golden age of Dutch art:
Dutch painters not only produced great art, they contributed to a
radical transformation in the European understanding of the nature
of art. However, it is now becoming clear that innovatory realistic art
was only a part of the total production of Dutch painters in this period.
From the late eighteenth century onwards, both private and institutional collectors saw Dutch realism as the best of the art produced in the
seventeenth century, and they selected paintings of this sort for preservation and public display. Realist art also came to be seen as an
expression of Dutch national character, and thus as an important part
of the national heritage.[3] In consequence, much of what Dutch artists
actually produced during the seventeenth century was neglected as
derivative, untypical of the national spirit, and thus unworthy of collection or of being displayed in major art galleries. In fact, Dutch artists
worked in a much wider range of styles than used to be assumed, and
in particular they produced a great number of paintings which were in
accord with the conventional conceptions of art prevalent in the rest of
Europe at that time. Much effort has gone into the reinterpretation of
Dutch 'realistic' art to try to show that such paintings had in fact a
conventional iconographic content and thus were not simply realistic;
this disputed enterprise has been perhaps less useful than the simple
revelation that there was more to Dutch seventeenth-century art than
was revealed by the collections of the Rijksmuseum in Amsterdam or
the National Gallery in London.

The growth of a realistic school of art in the seventeenth century with
its emphasis on a range of fairly new and unconventional subjects –
landscape, seascape, townscape, genre and so on – has to be related to
the changing nature of the market for art in the Republic, and especially in Holland. Economic growth and urban expansion greatly
increased the size, certainly absolutely and probably relatively as well,
of the middling groups in Dutch society, and it was the middle and
lower middle classes with modest amounts of surplus income which
provided a new and buoyant market for Dutch painters. What they
needed was relatively cheap paintings – they were after all not rich –
suitable in size and subject matter to be hung in the home. They were

in the main protestant and thus not in the market for traditional religious themes,[4] and perhaps had rather unsophisticated tastes in art. What evidence there is suggests that they bought their paintings from dealers and street markets, rather than through individual commissions to selected artists.

The nature of this particular market determined the size, subject matter and treatment of the art designed to appeal to its tastes and needs. The fact that such paintings were to be hung in private houses clearly put an upper limit on their size, moreover the evidence suggests that it was common practice to have many paintings in the same room and this was a further reason to keep them quite small. The placing of paintings in the common living space restricted their subject matter; many standard classical or religious themes might well have been considered unsuitable for family viewing. Family portraits, landscape and genre were among the most popular subjects, and such paintings were certainly unlikely to cause offence or unease when displayed in the home.

However, if this new – at least in its size – and partly anonymous market stimulated the development of the Dutch realistic school with its emphasis on mundane subject matter, it must not be forgotten that other markets existed and these ensured the persistence of more conventional – in terms of subject and treatment – forms of art. Although a royal court was lacking and the Reformed Church could not replace the old church as a patron of art, there were nevertheless commissions from various public bodies and these often required history paintings along conventional lines to make suitable moral or political points: the works commissioned in the 1650s for the new town hall in Amsterdam were intended to illustrate themes connected with the history and government of the town and, more broadly, of Holland. Rembrandt's *Conspiracy of Claudius Civilis* (1661–2) was one such commission which appears to have gone wrong, as the artist's treatment of the Batavian rebels did not quite fit the bill as far as the Amsterdam regents were concerned. They must have expected a classically inspired depiction of civic virtue; what they got was a one-eyed ruffian in a ruined cloister surrounded by equally disreputable followers in what must have been a conscious flouting of the standard iconography. Considerable patronage also emanated from the courts of successive princes of Orange, and this too tended to favour the sort of art which in subject and treatment would serve to enhance the prestige of the stadhouders. The artists favoured were often foreign and, even in the case of Dutch artists, what was required of them was certainly not the superficially simple work of the realist school. On the other hand some official commissions stimulated the development of the group portrait such as the numerous civic militia pieces, and collective portraits such as Frans Hals' *Regentesses of the Old Men's Home* and Rembrandt's *Syndics of the Cloth Guild.*

Such commissions were relatively well paid, in contrast to the low prices for paintings which were the rule on the open market. Connoisseurs were also willing to pay high prices for works of art that suited their taste. Through education and expertise they were attuned to the canons of art appreciation prevalent in contemporary Europe, and they looked for a complex and subtle iconology in paintings as well as a refined technique. Such enthusiasts came from the more wealthy sections of Dutch society and were prepared to pay to pursue their interests, and they represented a ready market for genre paintings embodying highly complex symbolism, especially when combined with the technical virtuosity of a Gerrit Dou, for conventional history paintings, and for Italianate landscapes. So, while the vast expansion of the market for art in seventeenth-century Holland came at the realistic and cheap end, there was also a considerable demand for more expensive art of a more conventional nature. Dutch economic growth had increased the number of wealthy people who could afford to indulge in such luxuries, as well as creating a large middling group in society with enough money to buy cheap paintings. Recent, though somewhat speculative, calculations have stressed the enormous number of paintings produced by Dutch artists during this century[5] and the very large numbers of painters it took to produce them. Most of this production, however, would be of fairly poor quality, much of it low-grade copies, selling at very low prices. Most paintings were cheap and most painters had a low socio-economic status.

However, while vast numbers of cheap, and probably nasty, paintings were produced for the popular end of the market, it was this demand which stimulated the realism and the mundane subject matter which were the hallmarks of what came to be regarded as the Dutch School. So the taste of this new market for art helped to bring about a major innovation in the history of art. The painters who supplied this market were artisans who had served an apprenticeship, were members of a guild, and produced what would sell in order to earn an honest crust. Mostly they remained at a distinctly modest economic level. However, it is also true that appenticeship to an artist was relatively expensive,[6] and that a craftsman was also a businessman employing journeymen and apprentices. It was possible for a painter to become quite prosperous on the basis of a productive workshop,[7] and it would be a mistake to underestimate the economic position and potential of the individual artisan.[8] Nevertheless, there is evidence for a distinct overproduction of painters by about the middle of the century, and for most of them the pickings must have been rather lean.

While the growth of an anonymous market stimulated both the production of a large number of paintings and an essentially new type of art, other fine arts such as sculpture suffered from the absence of royal patronage, the economic weakness of the nobility, and the end of commissions from the church. Such conditions were not likely to support many sculptors, let alone a distinctive style of sculpture. On the other hand, the expansion of the towns of Holland did present opportunities for architecture and town planning: the concentric half-circles of canals which form the heart of modern Amsterdam are the most striking example of the creation of new forms of urban space in the seventeenth century, and its houses also show the exploitation of traditional domestic architecture with its characteristic stepped gables. Although the century produced a number of new town halls and other notable public buildings, including some churches specifically designed for protestant worship, it is not individual buildings but the *grachten* lined with houses of prosperous merchants and the towns themselves which constitute the most distinctive architectural legacy of the century.

In literature, the impact of the new market society is much less, or much less obvious. Literary production in this period seems to have remained firmly within the limits prescribed by contemporary European taste, and there is no literary equivalent of the realistic school of painting. However, the modern view of Dutch seventeenth-century literature has been distorted at least to some extent by generations of critics and commentators. The 'canon' was constructed in the last years of the eighteenth century and the first of the nineteenth and has remained essentially unchanged ever since,[9] but the principles of selection were very different from those which shaped the artistic canon. Fidelity to the ancients and to the principles exemplified in classical literature was still seen as essential to great writing, and so innovation in style or content was regarded with deep distrust. Anything which did not fit such stereotypes was omitted from the textbooks, and the picture of seventeenth-century literature which was subsequently presented was necessarily one which was firmly within the dominant European mode. Other forms of writing produced in the seventeenth century were neglected either as being poor literature or as not being literature at all. Modern categories as to what is and is not literature are not necessarily applicable to the past, and it may well be that what appears to be a puzzling conventionality in the Dutch literature of this period is very largely a result of a particular critical tradition. There may well be more variety and more innovation than reaches the textbooks.

However, there can be little doubt that those writers who came to be seen as the most important belonged to the conventional mainstream of European literature in terms of style, form and subject matter. Although it might be going too far to say that the leading Dutch writers simply echoed the values implicit in renaissance literature generally, there is an important sense in which their work failed to reflect the profound changes that were taking place in Dutch society. Hooft,[10] Huygens[11] and Vondel[12] looked to the classics, and to the renaissance interpretation of them, as their model of what literature should be. Cats[13] won his place in the canon through his apparent fidelity to the accepted rules, but now is seen to have a distinctive character as a moral mentor to the new bourgeois society though remaining at best a medi-ocre poet. This veneration for the classics was instilled by the educa-tional system: for those able to afford it the best education, whether provided by tutors at home or the Latin schools, was ancient history and literature, taught chiefly in Latin with some Ancient Greek added later. The prejudices created by such an education were made even more constricting by a culture which was essentially conservative. Whether in politics, religion or literature change was seen as corrup-tion or decay: Spanish rule had been criticised in terms of the original Batavian constitution, protestants called for a return to the early church, and writers were called upon to emulate the example of ancient writers. In such a conservative cultural climate, innovation in literature was likely to be seen as a deviation from the proper path of fidelity to universal and unchanging standards.

Writers educated in this way and sharing these values judged their own work and that of others according to the renaissance interpreta-tion of classical literature; even those, like Vondel, who had not enjoyed this education as a child or youth had to adopt its values if they were to be accepted by those who had. However, one innovation was permitted: they wrote in Dutch, following the development of literature in Italian, French and English since the fourteenth century, and they sought to make it a suitable vehicle for a literary culture to match that of the ancients. While moving away from the more extravagant claims that surfaced in the sixteenth century – such as that Dutch was the language of Eden – they sought to create a standard literary language which would at least bear comparison with French and Italian. Hooft and Huygens were prominent here and, though not everything they tried worked – the former's attempts to replace latinate words with neologisms from Dutch roots were not always successful – their writings showed that Dutch could indeed be a suitable medium for poetry and drama. These writers did not aim at a popular market nor, with the exception of Cats, did they gain one. They did not write for a living, but sought prestige, praise and perhaps influence among the richer and better educated minority which shared their tastes. The potential mass market did not affect this level of literature any more than it influenced history paintings.

Books were expensive, perhaps too expensive to encourage the development of a mass market, but there was a proliferation of popular literature at a different and, crucially, cheaper, level. From the early years of the Revolt onwards, there was a large and growing production of pamphlets commenting on current events; these ranged from cheap flysheets of a few pages to book-length publications, but what they had in common was the readiness to drop literary pretensions for an immediate impact on a wide audience. There seems also to have been a considerable popular demand for accounts of travels or adventures, particularly outside Europe, and for highly coloured or fantastic fictional narratives. Dutch society had a relatively high and growing literacy rate, and this created a potential market for such writings; the strength of the Dutch publishing industry did the rest. Writers may not have made a great deal of money from the sale of their books; publishing, on the other hand, flourished – there was certainly money to be made satisfying the needs of a broad reading public.

Of course, what was produced for popular consumption was not considered literature by contemporaries, and it has only recently attracted much attention. However, it is probably here that the roots of the more economic and direct prose style which triumphed in the eighteenth century must be sought. There was also a more demotic impulse to be heard in the comedies and farces of Bredero,[14] but he died young and the rather restricted audience for drama did not encourage innovation. There was only one permanent theatre in Amsterdam and few outside, and public performances were vulnerable to criticism from the Reformed Church and other guardians of public morals, a situation which encouraged caution in both writers and producers. Much of the literature produced for the popular market was by its nature ephemeral, but more has been lost sight of through a trick of critical perception which denied its existence as part of literature. However, it seems unlikely that any amount of literary detective work will discover the seventeenth-century novel. It is often said that the novel is the literary equivalent of bourgeois or capitalist society, yet the first recognised Dutch novels come only in the late eighteenth century. Why did the first bourgeois society not produce the novel in the seventeenth century, while ingenious scholars have found it in absolutist France?

The Dutch Republic was also a centre for innovation in a wide range of intellectual fields, but it is distinctly more problematical to construct plausible links between such developments and the social transformation of the century, though it is tempting to think that such links must exist. Certainly it was a relatively open society, with a censorship that was minimal in effect if not in intent, and this might be seen as congruous with the dominance of the market. A wider range of theological and philosophical issues could be discussed in public than in any other contemporary European state. Descartes published his most controversial work from the safety of the Republic, while he nervously awaited its reception in his native France, while Spinoza declared himself profoundly grateful to be able to live in a country which allowed such freedom of thought.[15] He was careful, however, not to publish during his lifetime that part of his work which most challenged the religious sensibilities of his time; he well knew that there were limits, if not to freedom of thought, then certainly to freedom of publication.

Religion was a particularly sensitive area and it was as well not to publish what might be considered atheistic or blasphemous to the conventional mind, at least not in one's own name. Political issues were also sensitive, and civil authorities at all levels introduced measures to limit what could be published.[16] Enforcement was a different matter, however, and the large number of printing presses in the country, together with the thorough-going decentralisation of political authority, made it difficult to track down the producers of illicit publications. In some cases one can suspect that the civil authorities were less than eager to prosecute those whose only crime was to have upset the all-too-easily disturbed ministers of the Reformed Church, and even in political matters what was anathema in one town might well be tolerated, if not encouraged, in another. Prosecutions mostly occurred in cases with direct or indirect political implications, or where the author or publisher failed to take the necessary precautions. Perhaps the most notorious example of the latter is Adriaen Koerbagh who published theologically provocative material under his own name, repeated the offence, and died in the Amsterdam *rasphuis*. More important than the actual prosecutions was the self-censorship by authors and publishers who knew the limits of the acceptable within Dutch society, but even taking this factor into account writers could publish more freely on sensitive religious and theological issues in the Republic than anywhere else in Europe.

Such a relative freedom also favoured the development of scientific thought; Galileo's discoveries could be published without fear of prosecution, though it has to be admitted that cartesian philosophy only made progress in the face of determined opposition from religious conservatives. Even in this case, however, the Reformed Church could only achieve an order from the States of Holland (1656) limiting the extent to which such ideas could be taught in the university of Leiden, and there was no ban on publication on the subject. In other respects, however, it is still difficult to trace convincing links between the peculiar social and economic development of the Republic and scientific change and innovation. It seems evident that there must be such a link but it remains elusive.[17] Of course, the technological needs of an expanding economy must have been a stimulus to scientific thought at a certain level: the improvements in windmill design were directly related to the boom in land drainage in the late sixteenth and early seventeenth centuries, while Christiaen Huygens' work on pendulums was part of the search for an improved chronometer to facilitate navigation at sea. Similarly, the army's specific needs led directly to the setting up of a school to train military engineers at the university of Leiden (with the teaching in Dutch as opposed to the usual Latin) under the inspiration of the mathematician, Simon Stevin, but this proved to be short-lived. An awareness of the practical utility of technological improvements may have helped to encourage the growth of a scientific spirit, but on the other hand there were no real technological breakthroughs in this period and most production techniques in shipbuilding and textiles, for example, were based on traditional methods and pragmatic rule-of-thumb developments rather than any direct application of science. The intensive trading and colonial connections between the Republic and the extra-European world brought a flow of new information as well as products for the market. The effects ranged from the introduction of tea and coffee, which rapidly become popular drinks (earlier the use of tobacco had also become, rather less benignly, very common), to the taste for curiosity cabinets among the wealthy in the later years of the century. Such contacts and specimens of new plants in particular encouraged research into the natural world, and although the possible medical uses of such plants were the first concern, more disinterested scientific interest followed.

The greater intellectual openness of Dutch society, and particularly the weakness of religious inhibitions on scientific thought, made the Republic one of the chief centres for the publication of new scientific works in Europe, and in itself this must have been a considerable stimulus to the development of the new ideas in the country. In the later part of the century learned periodicals published in the Republic but usually written in French or Latin, such as Pierre Bayle's *Nouvelles de la République des Lettres*, acted as the European clearing-house for new ideas in science as well as theology and philosophy. This kept Dutch thinkers in touch with developments elsewhere and also gave them the opportunity to propagate their ideas and discoveries. It is notable, however, that the Dutch failed to set up a national academy of sciences. That there was no Dutch equivalent of the Royal Society in England or the *Académie des Sciences* in France was perhaps one of the less fortunate results of the extreme political decentralisation of the country, but it meant that Leeuwenhoek publicised his work through the Royal Society while Christiaen Huygens worked for many years at the *Académie* in Paris.

Although the teaching of medicine at Dutch universities had a high reputation, which continued into the eighteenth century as personified in the figure of the internationally respected Herman Boerhaave, innovation in science very largely took place outside formal higher education. Although Stevin had, as we have seen, a peripheral involvement with Leiden, Huygens never had an academic post in the Republic and Leeuwenhoek held a minor local government office in Delft. There is a sense, however, in which the universities did provide some ideological support for the new scientific approach – there was rapid and enthusiastic support for cartesianism, and not just among philosophers. This movement was hindered but far from silenced by the agitation of theological conservatives. Also the innovatory work in

biblical scholarship and oriental languages within Dutch universities
was part of an ethos which was prepared to question accepted positions
even in sensitive areas. Not that there were not powerful conservative
forces in the Dutch universities – the new interpretations of scripture
came from linguists rather than theologians – but they did not win
every battle nor, perhaps, in the end, the war. It is somewhat easier to
suggest ways in which the peculiar conditions obtaining in the Republic
influenced or stimulated thought in other areas than the natural
sciences. The religious pluralism which existed in practice in the
Republic raised important issues about the nature and limits of toleration which concerned theology as well as political thought. In practice a
large degree of toleration seems to have been established by the last
years of the sixteenth century, but it has been suggested that it was only
the defeat of the remonstrants and their expulsion from the Reformed
Church that stimulated the elaboration – largely by remonstrant theologians – of a coherent theory of toleration.[18] Again perhaps as a
reflection of Dutch reality, such theories had distinct limitations; most
obviously, catholics were largely excluded from toleration, though the
emphasis was on the Catholic Church as an evil and dangerous institution rather than on individual catholics who tended to be regarded
rather as the victims of the oppression and deception of their own
church. Neither the need for a state church nor the dominance of the
Reformed Church were really brought into question, but this circum-
stance is as much a comment on political as religious thought. This
atmosphere may have helped to enable Dutch scholars to begin the task
of biblical reinterpretation in the light of better linguistic knowledge
and historical understanding, even to the extent of questioning some
protestant shibboleths. The identification of the papacy with antichrist,
for example, was undermined by Grotius among others by trying to
place the key biblical text, *Revelation*, in its historical context: they
argued that the antichrist referred to here was a roman emperor who
was persecuting christians in the first century, and thus the text should
not be interpreted as an eschatological prophecy. Such scholarship was
a major contribution to the interpretation of the New Testament in
particular, and arose from the combination of Dutch strength in classical and near-eastern linguistics with a society that was relatively tolerant
of ideas even if they had radical implications, especially if they were
published in the relative safety of Latin.

The economic changes of the time also brought into question some
important aspects of the traditional ethical teachings of the Christian

Church. An economic morality set out in the first centuries of the christian era and elaborated in the later middle ages was in many ways ill-suited to the emergent capitalist society of the seventeenth century, but it was difficult to distinguish those aspects of conventional thinking which were only appropriate to earlier economic systems from more fundamental christian values. This problem is exemplified by the controversy which surrounded the publication of a book on usury by the *émigré* huguenot, Salmasius, in 1638: he tried to modify the traditional condemnation of taking interest on money lent as exploitation of the needy; his arguments aroused considerable opposition, though it now seems obvious that such activities were an inescapable part of capitalism. Even in the fifth decade of the century the new society that was emerging in the Republic was still struggling with cultural standards inherited from an earlier age.

The particular problems of the new state stimulated developments in political theory, and history was also very largely used to comment on contemporary politics. The major question in the early years of the century was the nature and significance of the Revolt and of the new state which emerged from it. The dominant interpretation, exemplified in the quasi-official *De antiquitate reipublicae batavicae* (1610) of Grotius, attempted to minimise, indeed deny, the revolutionary nature of the break with Spain: Philip II had attempted to subvert the fundamental liberties of the people of the Netherlands, and the rising was a reassertion of the traditional political system, not an innovation. Going somewhat against this grain was a religious interpretation of the Revolt which stressed its providential purpose but fitted in badly with the internal pluralism and external pragmatism of the Republic. The crisis which arose from the remonstrant/contraremonstrant clash left a lasting mark on political attitudes and became entangled with the dispute between orangists and republicans over the location of leadership in the state. Until mid century, however, such controversies were fought out in markedly conservative terms: not only was past practice systematically seen as by definition correct, but the theoretical terms of the debate were equally conventional.

Only with the brothers Johan and Pieter de la Court does a more radical element emerge in Dutch political controversy. On the basis of a self-conscious cartesian rationalism, they were prepared to contend for the superiority of the political system of the Republic – as well as to deny the princes of Orange any justifiable place within it. However, despite the provocative writings of such radicals, much of Dutch political thinking continued to be on conventional lines, and even the De la Courts owed a greater debt to the established republican tradition than perhaps they realised.[19] Those elements in the Dutch experience in this century – a far-reaching degree of religious toleration and the first decisive steps towards the secularisation of political life – which might have been expected to promote a parallel renovation of thought about the nature and purpose of the state, were pragmatic responses to new challenges, and theoretical justification lagged far behind the practice. The true exception to this theoretical blandness is Spinoza, a doubly marginal character as a jew in a christian society who was expelled from his own community for heresy. His political philosophy can be directly related to the nature and problems of the Dutch state but, while clearly working in the republican tradition, he was typically corrosive of comfortable assumptions within this discourse, and his prescriptions moved in a distinctly democratic direction.[20]

Apart from formal political writings, works of history on the one hand, and a flood of pamphlets on the other were also modes of commenting on the proper nature of the Dutch state. The importance placed on historical precedent meant that history was an obvious place for political battles to be fought: the authority of Philip II was challenged by a particular reading of the history of the Netherlands since the time of the Batavians; and the influence of the princes of Orange supported or attacked by partial versions of Dutch history since the Revolt. Also pamphlets often took on an historical form, though most of them were too tied up with the quarrels of the moment to have much time for analytical depth. With all their faults, however, these ephemera of political comment are probably the best indications we have of how Dutch people outside regent circles understood their state and its politics; on a more generous scale, the works of history project contemporary assumptions into the past, and so contribute to our understanding of Dutch political consciousness.

There was a tension in Dutch culture which arose from the persistence of traditional modes and perceptions in a context of rapid social change; this lack of a comfortable fit between inherited norms and emergent realities can be exemplified most clearly perhaps in religion and education, but it was pervasive. In religion, conservative assumptions regarding the virtue and necessity of religious unity clashed with the unavoidable reality of religious pluralism. In education the values of classical antiquity were held up for admiration although, even in

their renaissance translation, their relevance to the Dutch situation in
the seventeenth century is far from self-evident. More generally, there
seems to be a pervasive incongruity between a rapidly changing society
and a culture which was still largely rooted in a world dominated by
noble perceptions and values. Although there is clear evidence of new
forms and attitudes in art, literature and religion, there is no self-
conscious espousal of bourgeois as against noble values. There was
nothing to parallel the French attack on 'feudalism', as a shorthand
term for all that was wrong with the old order, in the following century.[21] On the other hand, there was precious little feudalism, in the
more precise sense, to attack in the Republic in any case: the growth of
commerce and the power of the towns had long given the Netherlands
a distinctive cultural signature, marked by the adaptation of traditional
forms to changing needs and perceptions. However, the towns of the
Netherlands in the later middle ages had been small islands in an
aristocratic sea, and the Republic was a small country in a Europe still
dominated by noble values; in neither case was total cultural and
spiritual apartheid possible, especially as in both cases these were
commercial societies necessarily wide open to influences from outside.

It is almost impossible to discover how most Dutch people thought
and felt about religion, but the indications we have suggest a profound
ambivalence. There seems to have been a general acceptance of the fact
of religious diversity, together with a distaste for persecution. There is
little evidence of tension between catholic and reformed in the towns,
and protestant nonconformists seem to have aroused little apprehen-
sion in the population at large. Yet this was not a secularised society and
the idea of religious unity was still powerful: the disputes between
remonstrants and their opponents aroused deep anxieties in the population at large, and the persecution of the remonstrants after their
defeat in 1618–19 showed that, for the orthodox at least, the dream
of religious uniformity and community, even if it needed to be imposed
by force, had not died. The movement for a further reformation (*nadere
reformatie*) within the Reformed Church and the continuing passion to
impose the values of the public church on society as a whole were
together a powerful undertone in Dutch culture, balancing the tolerance and pluralism which pragmatism required. The Reformed ministers who poured out jeremiads against the insolence of the papists and
the poison of sectarian influences were not just the futile anachronisms
they too often appear; they were the voice of those who refused in the
name of religion to accept an easy compromise with the values that

were coming to dominate their society. Quite how important this section of the Dutch community was is difficult to say, but its existence
helps to explain why there were distinct limits to the degree of religious
toleration which could be allowed in the Republic.

The standard humanist education was designed to inculcate the
values of the classical world as understood in the Renaissance, and it
was left to the individual to determine what their relevance was for a
society very different both from the classical world and from Renaissance Italy. The classical curriculum was the core of education in
Europe from the Renaissance to the twentieth century, its teachings
were regarded as of universal validity rather than being time-bound,
and there is no evidence that contemporaries saw any incompatibility
between them and the emergent capitalist society of Holland. Only the
relatively wealthy, however, could afford such an education in the Latin
schools or by private tutors. A humanist education was evidence of
membership of the social élite, and command of the classical heritage
was the necessary qualification for being recognised as one of the
educated. Vondel found it necessary to learn Latin and demonstrate
his classical credentials as an adult in order to gain full recognition as a
poet and playwright by contemporary arbiters of taste.

Humanism embodied the social values of the ancient world – or at
least what humanists thought were those values. However, the humanists read the classical heritage as a body of ideas and precepts which
reinforced rather than challenged the prevailing assumptions of their
time. The most startling example of such a transformation was the way
in which the literature of the pagan world was made seamlessly compatible with christianity; the renaissance humanists simply do not seem
to have understood how different from their own the perceptions of
ancient writers were. Similarly, the social values of the educated élite
were read into the classics, and so the literature of the ancient world
came to be read as confirming the values of a society largely dominated
by noble landowners. In this way humanism could become the preferred method of training the élites of sixteenth- and seventeenth-
century Europe. It might be thought that the rapidly changing society
of the Dutch Republic embodied other values than those which could
be found in ancient literature even in its renaissance interpretation, but
a form of education concentrating on the classics was eagerly embraced
here by those who could afford it, and among the regents at least its
hold only grew in the course of the seventeenth century. In consequence, through their education the social and political élite of the

Republic were to a significant extent made part of a common European culture based essentially on a noble value system. Of course, only a very small minority of the population could enjoy this privileged schooling and most of the population could aspire to little more than the basic literacy taught in the schools for this purpose which were available almost everywhere. Also, tuition in other practical skills such as modern languages and mathematics was widely available, as well as apprenticeships and specialised training for business and seamanship.

Nevertheless, it is surely of some significance that the socially dominant group were imbued with a culture which had so little respect for commercial or entrepreneurial activities. The regents could and did derive a sense of public service from the civic humanism of the renaissance, but there was always a certain ambivalence between the stress on honour in humanist teachings and the hunt for profit inherent to an active business life. That contemporaries should have shown so little awareness of such a clash of values is equally intriguing. At the very least the regent retreat from active involvement with trade or manufactures which was becoming evident in the later years of the century can only have been encouraged by an education which was less than appreciative of commercial values.

However, the widespread availability of basic schooling helped to make the Republic perhaps the most literate society in Europe at the time and, even for women, the proportion able to read and write grew rapidly in the course of the century. At the other extreme, although the new universities founded in the Republic after the Revolt built their reputations on calvinist theology and by continuing the high standards of Netherlands' humanism, they also proved themselves capable of significant innovation. The study of law showed a fresh approach within an established discipline, and by the later years of the century the political implications of the work of men like Gerard Noodt foreshadowed the Enlightenment if not liberalism.[22] Biblical scholarship also flourished, though through the work of linguists not theologians, and can be seen as laying down the groundwork for modern hermeneutics; and the Dutch medical faculties quickly gained a reputation as the most advanced in Europe, bringing into question the authority of the standard authors, partly through the use of dissection to correct their anatomical errors. However, the traditional, indeed the conservative, still dominated and not only in the faculties of theology; cartesianism was taken up with enthusiasm by Dutch thinkers, but there were restrictions on the extent to which it could be taught in the universities.

There were considerable variations from province to province, even region to region, with the hand of the past lying considerably more heavily on the land provinces than on Holland, but even the latter showed stronger hangovers from the past than is immediately apparent. Here the traditional culture was heavily eroded by the end of the seventeenth century, but the breaking of the spell was a slower process than might have been expected.[23] The emergent secular values had to be expressed in ways that made them compatible with the still dominant religious ethos of Dutch society, and the early enlightenment – and even the Enlightenment proper – had to take on an explicitly christian form. Similarly, there was little in the way of an explicit attack on inherited values in favour of the more secular and pragmatic moral standards suitable for a commercial society. At all levels of society, bourgeois culture was powerful and even perhaps dominant, but it was in structural conflict with more traditional ways of thought and perception. The old values were still vigorously proclaimed while the new were implicit in action and choice rather than explicitly championed, and the extent to which the two sets of values were incompatible was perhaps only vaguely recognised. Similarly, although the dominance of the nobility, both political and social, had been decisively broken – at least in Holland – by the end of the seventeenth century, there was no very clear attack on the nobles and the social values they represented, and their prestige remained largely unchallenged. Although the suggestion that by the end of the century the regents as a group were beginning to ape the nobles and starting to form a new aristocracy themselves no longer carries much conviction, it is perhaps more important to note that they never represented themselves as a coherent alternative to noble rule. The regent oligarchy was politically and socially ambivalent: part of its title to legitimacy lay in the extent to which it was recruited from and represented the interests of the bourgeoisie, but there were also quasi-aristocratic assumptions in the claims of leading families to a right to political authority. These latter elements may even have increased in the course of the seventeenth century as the regents became more absorbed in government and less in business. In any case, the seventeenth century saw no such wholesale attack on the nobility and its values as was to happen elsewhere in the course of the Enlightenment.

One area where cultural change is most evident is witchcraft – or rather the way in which Dutch society responded to fears concerning witchcraft and accusations of *maleficia*. This topic has the advantage of being the subject of penetrating recent research and so can be used as an example of, on the one hand, the rapidity and extent of cultural change in the Republic and, on the other, of the less well-publicised persistence of more traditional attitudes and beliefs. The picture is not a simple one: although some parts of the Republic proved almost immune to the witchcraze, others most certainly were not; and, although the prosecution of witches ended here earlier than anywhere else in Europe, belief in the reality of witchcraft persisted at all levels of society. The Republic's reputation for a 'rational' and modern response to the supposed supernatural attack on Christian society is not entirely deserved; as might be expected, the Republic shared to a great extent the religious and philosophical views dominant in the rest of Europe which not only made witchcraft plausible, but made the denial of satanic power in the world something akin to heresy.[24] However necessary this reminder of the complexity of the situation, it should not be allowed to obscure the main point which is that the witch craze touched the Republic only very lightly and persecution of suspected witches had ended in most of the country by the early seventeenth century, when some of the worst outbreaks of the panic were still to come in France, the Holy Roman Empire and elsewhere – even England.

The political and administrative decentralisation of the Republic, especially the absence of a central appeal court, allowed marked differences to develop in the various provinces as regards the reaction to witchcraft accusations. Also, as has been suggested, the areas with the most rapid economic and social development seem to have been both least troubled by the phenomenon and able to shake it off earliest. In detail the picture is complex, but the overall pattern is tolerably clear. Holland, Zeeland and, in the main, Friesland, saw relatively few prosecutions and fewer executions for witchcraft in the sixteenth century, and there were (probably) no further judicial killings after the 1590s.[25] Indeed, so complete was the transformation in atmosphere, that most cases involving accusations of witchcraft in Holland in the following century seem to have been suits for slander against the accusers, actions which were too liable to backfire to be a good risk in much of the rest of Europe. Even in the church courts, the chief concern appears to have been the restoration of peace within the congregation rather than the pursuit of supposed witches.[26] By the beginning of the seventeenth century, the authorities in these more developed areas were no longer prepared to prosecute alleged witches, and it is clear that informed opinion – notably medical – had turned against such trials. However, it is far from clear to what extent this change also reflected a lessening of fears of witchcraft in society at large. On the one hand there is plenty of evidence for the persistence of belief in witchcraft, but it may well be that such beliefs were neither so strong nor so central to most people's perception of the world around them as elsewhere. In an increasingly commercial – and prosperous – society, people's material existence was increasingly determined by fluctuations in the economy – unpredictable perhaps but hardly magical – rather than crop failures and the like which could all too easily be attributed to witchcraft. Even in the countryside of Holland, capitalist farmers were more attuned to the market than to rumours of supernatural malevolence. By the eighteenth century even the devastating cattle plagues may have been seen as an act of god but they were no longer blamed on witches.

In contrast, in other parts of the Republic relatively severe persecution of accused witches continued well into the seventeenth century. In Groningen the lack of a provincial court of appeal meant that local witch panics could go unchecked. Gelderland and North Brabant were strongly influenced by neighbouring regions of the Spanish Netherlands and the Holy Roman Empire, and campaigns against witchcraft which were severe by Dutch standards continued into the seventeenth century. Moreover, in these regions it would seem that, even after the prosecutions had ceased, belief in the reality of witchcraft and fears of its effects remained more central to people's lives than in the west of the country.[27] In general, though the picture is complicated by political, religious and geographic circumstances, the link between socio-economic development and the ending of witchcraft prosecutions seems inescapable.

Even in those regions of the Republic where witchcraft prosecutions and small-scale panics were still taking place in the early decades of the century, they had more or less died out by the middle of the seventeenth century. However, in common with the rest of Europe, trials for witchcraft ended in the Republic before belief in witches was generally discredited. The judicial authorities throughout Europe, though notably earlier in Holland than elsewhere, lost confidence in the judicial process with regard to witchcraft, partly because of a number of spectacular miscarriages of justice, but more generally because of well-founded doubts as to whether those being tried and convicted were indeed witches. Judges, lawyers and their advisers continued to believe in the reality of witchcraft but not that the accused who appeared in their courts were in fact witches.[28] In Holland a decision by the provincial court of appeal in the 1590s in effect rejected evidence obtained by torture, and helped to make conviction in witchcraft cases very difficult. This was evidence of, and was reinforced by, increasing scepticism in legal and medical circles regarding the guilt of those who actually came before the courts. However, conventional opinion continued to regard belief in the reality of satanic activity in this world as required by belief in god; denial of the existence of witchcraft and witches was seen by theologians and ministers of the official church as tantamount to atheism. As late as 1691, Balthasar Bekker, a minister of the Reformed Church in Amsterdam, came under general attack and was suspended by the North Holland synod for his publication of *De betoverde wereld* (*The Bewitched World*), which attacked witchcraft beliefs and argued that Satan's powers in the world had come to an end with the coming of Christ. By this time, however, educated opinion had shifted decisively: Bekker's salary continued to be paid by the town government of Amsterdam, and his mild scepticism was clearly in tune with the atmosphere of the early enlightenment in the Republic. Even the Reformed Church, though it clung to its theoretical belief in witchcraft, on the evidence of church court records, does not seem to have been too concerned with it in practice. Popular magical beliefs persisted, but possibly at a lower level of intensity, at least in the commercialised society of the maritime regions, while the educated came increasingly to see such ideas as evidence of backwardness.

Changes in the response to witchcraft accusations and the erosion of magical beliefs, at least among the educated, are evidence of the profound cultural changes that were taking place in the Republic by the early years of the century if not earlier. Here again, however, changes in practice are more evident than any theoretical challenge to prevailing ideas. There was a tradition of scepticism in the Netherlands with regard to witchcraft which stretched back at least as far as Johan Wier in the sixteenth century but, apart from Bekker, the record of such publications in the seventeenth century does not seem to have been very impressive. Evidently, a theologically based denial of witchcraft beliefs in principle was considerably more problematic than a robust scepticism in judicial practice. Again, with all the variations in time and place which have been mentioned, the Republic nevertheless stands out for its resistance to ideas of a satanic conspiracy against Christendom, and it ceased to burn people as witches long before the rest of Europe freed itself from this particularly vicious aspect of the magical universe.

It has been argued in this chapter that there were both profound divisions and deep ambivalences in Dutch culture in the seventeenth century. The rapid changes taking place in the maritime provinces were balanced by the much greater conservatism of the land provinces; while the emergence of a recognisably modern, secular society was contradicted by the persistence of traditional mentalities. The conflict between a Reformed Church which sought to impose its own values on society as a whole and the broadly tolerant policies of the political authorities almost everywhere in the Republic is a prime example of the underlying tensions in Dutch society. The conventional picture of a tolerant and humane society is being replaced by an account which places more stress on the considerable limitations on this much-vaunted toleration. Perhaps this is an overly cynical reaction: a greater awareness of the obstacles on the path to toleration should make us more appreciative of what was in fact achieved rather than less. More generally, the tension between traditional values and perceptions and the emergent new culture can be seen as a stimulus to innovatory solutions, not just as a cause of conflict. It might also be argued that such problems were not entirely new to the region.

The new culture that was emerging in the Republic in the seventeenth century had its roots in the urban culture of the Netherlands in the previous century and perhaps even in the later middle ages. There is clearly a genetic relationship between the relatively tolerant religious attitudes of Netherlands' humanists from the early sixteenth century onwards and those of the liberal protestants of the later seventeenth. Similarly, both the literary and artistic developments of the Golden Century were marked, for better or worse, by their inheritance from the pre-Revolt urban culture. So, if this was an urbanised and capitalist society built on a conservative culture, this latter was at least a culture which had been softened up by a century or more of urban dominance and commercial priorities. Also the degree of change should not be exaggerated: even in Holland local variations were important, and the old order may have survived better in some of the smaller towns than in the bigger cities, while the forces for cultural transformation were probably also less strong in those towns which experienced economic problems early on in the century. If Holland was not a scene of mono-lithic modernisation, neither were the other provinces simply tradition-alist. Economically the whole of the Republic was drawn into the market system driven by Holland, and this process inevitably had cultural as well as social consequences. It was only in comparison with the leading province that these regions seemed conservative; on a European scale the extent to which they were changing is more apparent. The early cessation of witch trials in most of the land provinces is at least as significant as their continuation into the first decades of the seventeenth century and by the end of the century there is some evidence that cultural leadership was beginning to move away from Holland and towards the old cultural centres to the east.[29]

Finally, there were distinct limits to the degree to which Dutch culture could break away from the norms of Europe as a whole. At all levels the Dutch were part of a broader European cultural system[30] and shared its values to a considerable extent. The élite were formed by the same classically based education, with its deeply conservative implications, as the rest of Europe and, on a more popular level, the Dutch shared the religious beliefs and prejudices which prevailed at the time. There was a limit to which a small country – and especially a small country which was intensely involved with the rest of Europe because of its dependence on trade – could free itself from the hegemony of common cultural attitudes. The cultural changes that took place in the Dutch Republic in the seventeenth century were considerable, but in the end it may well have been impossible for a fully bourgeois society and culture to emerge in one country, especially when that country was not only small but itself divided between modernising and more conservative forces.

NOTES AND REFERENCES

INTRODUCTION

1. The classic expression of an historical Belgian identity ante-dating the creation of the state can be found in Henri Pirenne, *Histoire de Belgique (1899–1932)*, while the (rather less classic) Dutch counterpart is P.J. Blok, *Geschiedenis van het Nederlandsche Volk (1892–1907)*.
2. This was a major theme of the work of Pieter Geyl, who was particularly concerned that what he saw as the essential unity of all Dutch-speaking people had been disrupted in the course of the Revolt. See, e.g., *The Revolt of the Netherlands* (London, 1958).
3. See James D. Tracy, *A Financial Revolution in the Habsburg Netherlands* (Berkeley, CA, 1985) and *Holland under Habsburg Rule, 1506–66* (Berkeley, CA, 1990), also J.W. Koopmans, *De staten van Holland en de Opstand* (The Hague, 1990).
4. See Martin van Gelderen, *The Political Thought of the Dutch Revolt* (Cambridge, 1993).
5. Usually – though misleadingly, at least at this time – referred to by historians as calvinist.
6. See below, Chapter 4.
7. Named after Menno Simons, they represented a pacifist tendency among the broader anabaptist movement.
8. J.I. Israel, *Dutch Primacy in World Trade* (Oxford, 1989), ch. 3.
9. *Pace* the advocates of an economic crisis of the 1590s, e.g. Peter Clark (ed.), *The European Crisis of the 1590s* (London, 1985).
10. Jan de Vries, *The Dutch Rural Economy in the Golden Age 1500–1700* (New Haven, CT, 1974) was a pioneer work in arguing for the central importance of the rural sector for Dutch economic growth in this period.
11. Even in industrialising England this degree of urbanisation was not reached until the middle of the nineteenth century – 300 years after Holland.
12. Originally the legal adviser of the States of Holland, by this period this post was becoming the most powerful political office in the province.
13. That is, legal counsel to the government of the town.
14. See below, Chapter 3.
15. See below, Chapter 4.
16. Jonathan I. Israel, *The Dutch Republic. Its Rise, Greatness and Fall 1477–1806* (Oxford, 1995).

17. Pieter Geyl, *The Netherlands in the Seventeenth Century*, 2 vols (London, 1961–4).

18. K.H.D. Haley, *The Dutch in the Seventeenth Century* (London, 1972).

1 THE IMPACT OF A NEW STATE IN EUROPE

1. For a sympathetic treatment of Leicester's career in the Netherlands, see F.G. Oosterhoff, *Leicester and the Netherlands 1586–87* (Utrecht, 1988).

2. J.L. Price, 'A State Dedicated to War? The Dutch Republic in the Seventeenth Century', in *The Medieval Military Revolution*, ed. Andrew Ayton and J.L. Price (London, 1995), pp. 183–200.

3. These were duties imposed by Denmark on trade entering and leaving the Baltic.

4. For the problems which arose with England from Dutch attempts to enforce this blockade, see S. Groenveld, *Verlopend getij* (Dieren, 1984).

5. The Dutch East India Company (*Vereenigde Oostindische Compagnie*).

6. See J.L. van Zanden, *The Rise and Decline of Holland's Economy. Merchant Capitalism and the Labour Market* (Manchester, 1993), pp. 71–9.

7. See below, Chapter 3.

8. Cf. J.L. Price, *Holland and the Dutch Republic in the Seventeenth Century* (Oxford, 1994), Part 3.

9. As in G. Parker, 'Why did the Dutch Revolt Last So Long?', in *Spain and the Netherlands 1559–1659* (London, 1979), p. 63.

10. Golo Mann, *Wallenstein* (Frankfurt am Main, 1971), pp. 499–505; M.E.H.N. Mout, '"Holendische Propositiones". Een Habsburg plan tot vernietiging van handel, visserij en scheepvaart der Republiek (ca. 1625)', *Tijdschrift voor Geschiedenis*, 95:3 (1982), 345–62.

11. Cf. R.J. Evans, *The Making of the Habsburg Monarchy 1550–1700* (Oxford, 1979), ch. 6.

12. A good example of the confusion in perceptions of national interest which could arise from the conflict between ideological sympathy and other motives can be found in the disagreements over English foreign policy in the 1620s and 1630s, cf. S. Adams, 'Spain or the Netherlands? The Dilemmas of Early Stuart Foreign Policy', in H. Tomlinson (ed.), *Before the English Civil War* (London, 1983); L.J. Reeve, *Charles I and the Road to Personal Rule* (London, 1989), ch. 7.

13. However, the Dutch part in the Thirty Years War has never been comprehensively studied, and remains underplayed in G. Parker (ed.), *The Thirty Years War* (London, 1984), but cf. J.I. Israel, *The Dutch Republic and the Hispanic World, 1606–1661* (Oxford, 1982). J.V. Polisensky, *The Thirty Years War* (London, 1971), ch. 5, gives rather more consideration to the Dutch, see also the same author's *Tragic Triangle. The Netherlands, Spain and Bohemia 1617–1621* (Prague, 1991).

14. See below, Chapter 4.

15. See below, Chapter 2.

16. Cf. R. Stradling, *The Armada of Flanders: Spanish Maritime Policy and European War, 1568–1668* (Cambridge, 1992); R. Baetens, 'The organization

and effects of Flemish privateering in the seventeenth century', *Acta Historiae Neerlandicae*, 9 (1976), 48–75.

17. The Dutch swapped New Netherland (New York) for Surinam, which seemed like a good deal at the time.

18. R. Liesker, 'Tot zinkens toe bezwaard. De schuldenlast van het Zuiderkwartier van Holland 1672–1794', in *Bestuurders en geleerden*, ed. S. Groenveld, M.E.H.N. Mout and I. Schöffer (Amsterdam/Dieren, 1985), pp. 151–60.

19. Cf. P. Geyl, *Orange and Stuart* (London, 1969), originally published in Dutch in 1939.

20. J.I. Israel, however, prefers to stress the economic motivations behind the Holland regents' decision to take a firmer line both against France and with regard to England at this time, see 'The Dutch role in the Glorious Revolution', in *The Anglo- Dutch Moment*, ed. J.I. Israel (Cambridge, 1991), esp. pp. 110–19.

21. The most up-to-date study is H.L. Zwitzer, *'De militie van den staat'. Het leger van de Republiek der Verenigde Nederlanden* (Amsterdam, 1991).

22. J.R. Bruijn, *The Dutch Navy in the Seventeenth and Eighteenth Centuries* (Colombia, SC, 1993).

23. Price, 'A State Dedicated to War?'

24. J. Heringa, *De eer en hoogheid van de staat. Over de plaats der Verenigde Nederlanden in het diplomatieke leven van de zeventiende eeuw* (Groningen, 1961), p. 263.

25. See C.R. Boxer, *The Dutch in Brazil, 1624–54* (Oxford, 1957).

2 THE ECONOMIC MIRACLE – AND ITS LIMITATIONS

1. Indispensable to any discussion of the Dutch economy in this period is now Jan de Vries and Ad van der Woude, *The First Modern Economy. Success, Failure, and Perseverance of the Dutch Economy, 1500–1815* (Cambridge, 1997).

2. The use of this concept – merchant capitalism – is criticised in De Vries and Van der Woude, *The First Modern Economy*, pp. 690–3, principally because they see it as obfuscating the 'modern' character of the Dutch economy in the early modern period.

3. De Vries and Van der Woude, pp. 46–52.

4. J.I. Israel, *Dutch Primacy in World Trade* (Oxford, 1989), pp. 379 ff. It should be noted that Israel is concerned primarily with trade, not the economy as a whole.

5. J. Bieleman, *Boeren op het Drentse zand* (Wageningen, 1987), esp. pp. 665–71, shows how profoundly the Amsterdam market affected the agrarian economy of this relatively poor region.

6. De Vries and Van der Woude, *The First Modern Economy*, pp. 244–5, 249–50.

7. J.L. van Zanden: *The Rise and Decline of Holland's Economy. Merchant Capitalism and the Labour Market* (1993), pp. 30–1.

8. Jan De Vries, *The Dutch Rural Economy in the Golden Age, 1500–1700* (New Haven, CT, 1974).

9. The *randstad* (rim-town) is a term which regards the urbanised areas of Holland between roughly Rotterdam in the south and Amsterdam in the north as, in an important sense, acting as a single city.

10. Cf. E.A. Wrigley, *Continuity, Chance and Change: the Character of the Industrial Revolution in England* (Cambridge, 1988), p. 49.

11. De Vries and Van der Woude, *The First Modern Economy*, pp. 353, 372.

12. Israel tends to underplay its importance, see *Dutch Primacy*, pp. 8–11.

13. The classic work on this system is T.P. van der Kooy, *Hollands stapelmarkt en haar verval* (Amsterdam, 1931).

14. The French minister Colbert estimated the Dutch merchant fleet at 20 000 ships: J.L. Price, *Culture and Society in the Dutch Republic during the Seventeenth Century* (London, 1974), p. 43.

15. Much depends, of course, on definition, particularly in the case of smaller ships.

16. R.A. Stradling, *The Armada of Flanders: Spanish Maritime Policy and European War, 1568–1668* (Cambridge, 1992); R. Baetens, 'The organization and effects of Flemish privateering in the seventeenth century', *Acta Historiae Neerlandicae*, 9 (1976), 48–75; but see also J.R. Bruijn, 'Dutch privateering during the Second and Third Anglo-Dutch Wars', *The Low Countries History Yearbook* 1978/ *Acta Historiae Neerlandicae*, 11 (1978), 79–93.

17. Cf. Jan de Vries, *Barges and Capitalism. Passenger Transportation in the Dutch Economy (1632–1839)* (Wageningen, 1978), pp. 19, 31–2; and on economic conflict between the towns of North Holland, particularly centring on transport by water, see Diederik Aten, 'Als het gewelt comt...'. *Politiek en economie in Holland benoorden het IJ, 1500–1800* (Hilversum, 1995).

18. A.M. van der Woude, *Het Noorderkwartier* (Wageningen, 1972), pp. 50–5.

19. De Vries and Van der Woude, *The First Modern Economy*, pp. 27–32.

20. See for the effects on a village in the Schermereiland, A. Th. Van Deursen, *Een dorp in de polder. Graft in de zeventiende eeuw* (Amsterdam, 1994), pp. 52–5.

21. V. Barbour, *Capitalism in Amsterdam* (Baltimore, MD, 1950) is still the classic study.

22. The classic contemporary statement of this resentment was Thomas Mun, *England's Treasure by Forraign Trade* (Oxford, 1959), pp. 74–81 (first published in 1664).

23. See Jan de Vries, *The Economy of Europe in an Age of Crisis* (Cambridge, 1976), ch. 1.

24. C.M. Cipolla, *Before the Industrial Revolution* (London, 1976), pp. 231–3.

25. Cf. G. Parker, 'War and Economic Change: the Economic Costs of the Dutch Revolt', in *Spain and the Netherlands* (London, 1979), pp. 178–203.

26. J.I. Israel, *Dutch Primacy*, pp. 198–201.

27. J. Lucassen, *Naar de kusten van de Noordzee. Trekarbeid in Europees perspektief 1600–1900* (Gouda, 1984); see also his, 'The North Sea: a crossroads for migrants?', in *The North Sea and Culture (1550–1800)*, ed. Juliette Roding and Lex Heerma van Voss (Hilversum, 1996), pp. 168–84.

28. Its importance has been stressed in numerous publications by J. Briels, including *De Zuid-Nederlandse immigratie 1572–1630* (Haarlem, 1978) and

Zuid-Nederlanders in de Republiek 1572–1630. Een demografische en cultuur-historische studie (Sint Niklaas, 1985).

29. Lotte C. van de Pol, 'The lure of the big city. Female migration to Amsterdam', in *Women of the Golden Age*, ed. Els Kloek, Nicole Teeuwen and Marijke Huisman (Hilversum, 1994), pp. 73–81.

30. See S. Hart, 'Onderzoek naar de samenstelling van de bevolking van Amsterdam in de 17e en 18e eeuw, op grond van gegevens over migratie, huwelijk, beroep en alfabetisme', in *Geschrift en getal* (Dordrecht, 1976), pp. 115–81.

31. The classic survey is still C.R. Boxer, *The Dutch Seaborne Empire* (London, 1965).

32. Israel, *Dutch Primacy*.

33. J.M. Postma, *The Dutch in the Atlantic Slave Trade 1600–1815* (Cambridge, 1990).

34. See F. Braudel, *Civilisation matérielle, économie et civilisation, 15e–18e siècle* (Paris, 1979), vol. 3, pp. 118–29, 145–6.

3 REPUBLICANISM IN PRACTICE

1. See on this question, J. L. Price, 'A State Dedicated to War? The Dutch Republic in the Seventeenth Century', in *The Medieval Military Revolution*, ed. Andrew Ayton and J.L. Price (London, 1995), pp. 183–200.

2. Not exactly, perhaps: its official title was the United Provinces of the Netherlands, but the republican implications of this were obvious and undisguised.

3. 'I much prefer a Republic, content with its possessions, seeking only to conserve them, and to secure for its inhabitants a tranquil and peaceful life.' Quoted in W.R.E. Velema, *Enlightenment and Conservatism in the Dutch Republic. The Political Thought of Elie Luzac (1721–1796)* (Assen/Maastricht, 1993), p. 70.

4. Sir William Temple, *Observations upon the United Provinces of the Netherlands*, ed. Sir George Clark (Oxford, 1972), p. 53; O. Mörke, 'Sovereignty and Authority. The role of the court in the Netherlands in the first half of the seventeenth century', Ronald G. Asch and Adolf M. Birke (eds), *Princes, Patronage, and the Nobility. The Court at the Beginning of the Modern Age (c. 1450–1650)* (Oxford, 1991), pp. 455–77.

5. Another victim of this mode of thinking has been the Holy Roman Empire which until recently has been conventionally seen as having no real existence as a state. Happily in recent years historians have begun to show more interest in it as a working political system.

6. J.L. Price, *Holland and the Dutch Republic in the Seventeenth Century. The Politics of Particularism* (Oxford, 1994), p. 285 and Part III in general.

7. J.L. Price, 'Restoration England and Europe', in *The Restored Monarchy, 1660–1688*, ed. J.R. Jones (London, 1979), p. 121.

8. Cf. Johannes Althusius, *Politica methodice digesta* (1603) which is essentially an analysis of the constitution of the Empire, but has also been used as a way of understanding the Dutch political system.

9.   Brian M. Downing, *The Military Revolution and Political Change* (Princeton, NJ, 1992), esp. pp. 74–83, presents a rather more subtle variation on this theme.

10. Drenthe was also in the Republic and largely autonomous but was never represented in the States General.

11. Price, *Holland*, pp. 215, 284–6.

12. Jonathan Israel, *The Dutch Republic* (Oxford, 1995), pp. 276–7, asserts that such incidents prove that provincial autonomy was not an effective rule of the Dutch political system. However, it is clear that majority voting in the States General was never accepted in principle nor could it be, given the disparity between the provinces.

13. H. Gerlach, *Het proces tegen Oldenbarnevelt en de 'Maximen in den Staet'* (Haarlem, 1965).

14. Marjolein 't Hart, 'The Dutch Republic: the urban impact on politics', in *A Miracle Mirrored. The Dutch Republic in European Perspective*, ed. Karel Davids and Jan Lucassen (Cambridge, 1995), pp. 58–9.

15. As constituent parts of the Holy Roman Empire, thus.

16. James D. Tracy, *Holland under Habsburg Rule 1506–1566* (Berkeley, CA, 1990); see also the remarks in J.I. Israel, *The Dutch Republic*, p. 16.

17. Cf. J.L. Price, 'The Dutch Nobility in the Seventeenth and Eighteenth Centuries', in *The European Nobilities in the Seventeenth and Eighteenth Centuries*, vol. 1: *Western Europe*, ed. H.M. Scott (London, 1995), pp. 85–6. The *ridderschappen* were formal organisations of the nobles of a province controlling their representation in the provincial estates. Their increasingly exclusive character was an important element in the general process of oligarchisation of Dutch politics in this period.

18. H. Feenstra, *De bloeitijd en het verval van de Ommelandse adel, 1600–1800* (Groningen, 1981).

19. In any case, members of the Council of State, although nominated by their provinces, were not regarded as representing them once appointed.

20. Originally they were the legal advisers of the *ridderschap*, and continued to act as its spokesman in the States.

21. See the discussion of this point in H.H. Rowen, *Johan de Witt: Grand Pensionary of Holland* (Princeton, NJ, 1978), pp. 137–41.

22. Only six towns had been regular members of the States before the Revolt – Dordrecht, Amsterdam, Leiden, Haarlem, Delft and Gouda – but twelve others were admitted in the decade after 1572. A number of towns in the Southern Quarter of Holland remained excluded for reasons which remain unclear.

23. H.F.K. van Nierop, *The Nobility of Holland. From Knights to Regents, 1500–1650* (Cambridge, 1993), pp. 203–7.

24. Price, *Holland*, pp. 173–8.

25. It must be admitted that not all historians see this episode as a failure for the prince, cf. H.H. Rowen, 'The Revolution that Wasn't: the Coup d'Etat of 1650 in Holland', *European Studies Review*, 4 (1974), 99–117.

26. Curiously, these two courts, the *Hof van Holland* and the *Hoge Raad*, were shared with Zeeland and were thus almost unique instances of effective supra-provincial institutions.

27. The tradition of urban revolt in the Netherlands is discussed in Marc Boone and Maarten Prak, 'Rulers, patricians and burghers: the Great and Little traditions of urban revolt in the Low Countries', in *A Miracle Mirrored*, ed. Davids and Lucassen, pp. 99–134.

28. P. Geyl, *Het stadhouderschap in de partijliteratuur onder De Witt* (Amsterdam, 1947).

29. Peter J.A.N. Rietbergen, 'Beeld en zelfbeeld. "Nederlandse identiteit" in politieke structuur en politieke cultuur tijdens de Republiek', *Bijdragen en Mededelingen betreffende de Geschiedenis der Nederlanden*, 107, 4 (1992), 635–56.

30. The post in Friesland, and often Groningen and Drenthe also, was held by a cadet branch of the house.

31. See G.N. van der Plaat, 'Lieuwe van Aitzema's kijk op het stadhouderschap in de Republiek', *Bijdragen en Mededelingen betreffende de Geschiedenis der Nederlanden*, 103 (1988), 341–72.

32. The Fries Nassaus clung on, however, and took over the family position in the Dutch state after the death of Willem III without legitimate issue.

33. H.H. Rowen, *The Princes of Orange. The Stadholders in the Dutch Republic* (Cambridge, 1988), chs 9, 11.

34. Despite the population rise, the size of the oligarchies remained the same; in some towns, indeed, it decreased in the course of the century.

35. See, for example, Craig E. Harline, *Pamphlets, Printing and Political Culture in the Early Dutch Republic* (Dordrecht, 1987).

36. However, Israel, *Dutch Republic*, p. vi, claims that a significant divide between north and south in the Netherlands already existed before the Revolt, but even he might hesitate to claim that North Brabant, for example, was naturally a part of the North.

37. M.P. Christ, *De Brabantsche Saecke. Het vergeefsche streven naar een gewestelijke status voor Staats-Brabant 1585–1675* (Tilburg, 1984).

38. One of Pieter de la Court's major works was indeed *Interest van Holland, ofte gronden van Hollands-welvaren (Amsterdam, 1662)*.

4 RELIGION, POLITICS AND TOLERATION

1. J. Spaans, *Haarlem na de Reformatie. Stedelijke cultuur en kerkelijk leven, 1577–1620* (The Hague, 1989), p. 104.

2. For a general introduction to the question, see R. Po-Chia Hsia, *Social Discipline in the Reformation. Central Europe 1550–1750* (London, 1989).

3. A.C. Duke, *Reformation and Revolt in the Low Countries* (London, 1990), pp. 291–3.

4. Cf. the arguments of P. Geyl in *History of the Low Countries: Episodes and Problems* (London, 1964), pp. 32–42.

5. H. Roodenburg, *Onder censuur. De kerkelijke tucht in de gereformeerde gemeente van Amsterdam, 1578–1700* (Amsterdam, 1990).

6. Cf. the suggestive study of Utrecht in this period, B. J. Kaplan: *Calvinists and Libertines. Confession and Community in Utrecht 1578–1620* (Oxford, 1995).

7.   For the providential interpretation of Dutch history see C. Huisman, *Neerlands Israel. Het natiebesef der traditioneel-gereformeerden in de achttiende eeuw* (Dordrecht, 1983).

8.   R. Dekker, *Holland in Beroering. Oproeren in de 17de en 18de eeuw* (Baarn, 1982), p. 39. There were a number in the eighteenth century, however.

9.   For a rather less sanguine view, see Anton van de Sande, 'Roomse buitenbeentjes in een protestantse natie? Tolerantie en antipapisme in Nederland in de zeventiende, achttiende en negentiende eeuw', Marijke Gijwijt-Hofstra (ed.), *Een schijn van verdraagzaamheid* (Hilversum, 1989), pp. 85–106.

10. Though the Rotterdam *vroedschap* was reported to be 'full of Arminians' (i.e. remonstrants) in the 1660s, see *Briefwisseling tusschen de gebroeders Van der Goes 1659–1673*, ed. C.J. Gonnet (Amsterdam, 1899), pp. 2, 321.

11. For a useful account in English, see Andrew C. Fix, *Prophecy and Reason. The Dutch Collegiants in the Early Enlightenment* (Princeton, NJ, 1991).

12. Cf. L. Kolakowski, *Chrétiens sans Eglise* (Paris, 1969), pp. 166–77.

13. R.G. Fuks-Mansfeld, *De Sefardim in Amsterdam tot 1795* (Hilversum, 1989), pp. 45, 52–3.

14. Ibid., p. 10.

15. Florike Egmond, *Underworlds. Organized Crime in the Netherlands 1650–1800* (Cambridge, 1993), ch. 6.

16. Quoted in K.L. Sprunger, *The Learned Doctor William Ames* (Urbana, IL, 1972), p. 58.

17. The *statencollege* was a special foundation to provide training for future ministers of the Reformed Church.

18. See Price, *Holland*, part III, ch. 2.

19. See Chapter 6.

20. Robin Briggs, *Witches and Neighbours. The Social and Cultural Context of European Witchcraft* (London, 1996), e.g. p. 186, in my view underestimates the significance of the very early ending of prosecutions in Holland and thus overlooks the latter's originality.

21. See, for example, W. de Blécourt, *Termen van toverij. De veranderende betekenis van toverij in Noord-Oost Nederland tussen de 16de en 20ste eeuw* (Nijmegen, 1990).

22. See Chapter 6.

23. It must be remembered that blasphemy was still a criminal offence, and it could be widely interpreted.

24. For example, the links between political and religious factionalism in Zeeland in the later part of the century related in M. van der Bijl, *Idee en Interest. Voorgeschiedenis, verloop en achtergronden van de politieke twisten in Zeeland en vooral in Middelburg tussen 1702 en 1715* (Groningen, 1981).

5   A BOURGEOIS SOCIETY?

1.   A useful introduction to a complex and often confusing controversy can be found in Peter Burke, 'The language of orders in early modern

Europe', in M. L. Bush (ed.), *Social Orders and Social Classes in Europe since 1500* (London, 1992), pp. 1–12.

2. See Jan de Vries, *The Dutch Rural Economy in the Golden Age 1500–1700* (New Haven, CT, 1974).

3. Discussed in Chapter 2.

4. Jan Bieleman, *Boeren op het Drentse zand 1600–1910* (Wageningen, 1987), pp. 665–9.

5. De Vries and Van der Woude, *The First Modern Economy*, pp. 507–21; and the evidence for North Holland in C.M. Lesger, *Hoorn als stedelijk knooppunt. Stedensystemen tijdens de late middeleeuwen en vroegmoderne tijd* (Hilversum, 1990), appendix F.

6. J.L. van Zanden, *The Rise and Decline of Holland's Economy. Merchant Capitalism and the Labour Market* (Manchester, 1993), pp. 39–40, 116.

7. De Vries and Van de Woude, *The First Modern Economy*, pp. 60–1.

8. See Diederik Aten, *'Als het gewelt comt...' Politiek en economie in Holland benoorden het IJ 1500–1800* (Hilversum, 1995), pp. 232–63, for examples from the Northern Quarter of Holland.

9. E. Taverne, *In't land van belofte: in de nieue stadt. Ideaal en werkelijkheid van de stadsuitleg in de Republiek 1580–1680* (Marssen, 1978), ch. 5.

10. De Vries and Van de Woude, *The First Modern Economy*, p. 406.

11. J.L. Price, 'A State Dedicated to War? The Dutch Republic in the Seventeenth Century', in *The Medieval Military Revolution*, ed. Andrew Ayton and J.L. Price (London, 1995), p. 189. The most recent assessment of Dutch army size is in H.L. Zwitzer, *'De Militie van den Staet'. Het leger van de Republiek der Verenigde Nederlanden* (Amsterdam, 1991), bijlage 1.

12. Jaap R. Bruijn, *The Dutch Navy of the Seventeenth and Eighteenth Centuries* (Columbia, SC, 1993), p. 131.

13. For interesting contributions to this subject in English, see Els Kloek *et al.* (eds): *Women of the Golden Age. An International Debate on Women in Seventeenth-century Holland, England and Italy* (Hilversum, 1994).

14. See the general coverage in O. Hufton, *The Prospect before Her. A History of Women in Western Europe*, vol. 1, *1500–1800* (London, 1995).

15. Lotte van de Pol, *Het Amsterdams hoerdom. Prostitutie in de zeventiende en achttiende eeuw* (Amsterdam, 1996).

16. Willem de Blécourt, *Termen van toverij* (Nijmegen, 1990) includes frequent references to the bewitching of milk and the like.

17. See the tentative conclusions in Els Kloek, *Wie hij zij, man of wijf* (Hilversum, 1990), pp. 57–66, 74–7.

18. A. Th. van Deursen, *Plain Lives in a Golden Age* (Cambridge, 1991), pp. 7–9.

19. Ibid., p. 10.

20. For an overview, see J.L. Price, 'The Dutch Nobility in the Seventeenth and Eighteenth Centuries', in H.M. Scott (ed.), *The European Nobilities in the Seventeenth and Eighteenth Centuries*, vol. 1: *Western Europe* (London, 1995), pp. 82–113.

21. H.F.K. van Nierop, *The Nobility of Holland: from Knights to Regents 1500–1650* (Cambridge, 1993).

6   A DIVIDED CULTURE

1. See the now classic work: C. Busken Huet, *Het land van Rembrandt* (Haarlem, 1882–4).

2. J.L. Price, *Culture and Society in the Dutch Republic during the Seventeenth Century* (London, 1974), esp. ch. 6, and, in a rather more nuanced way, Marten Jan Bok and Gary Schwartz, 'Schilderen in opdracht in Holland in de 17e eeuw', *Holland*, 23, 4/5 (1991), 183–95.

3. Frans Grijzenhout and Henk van der Veen, *De Gouden Eeuw in perspectief. Het beeld van de Nederlandse zeventiende- eeuwse schilderkunst in later tijd* (Nijmegen, 1992)

4. Though an intriguing possibility is that there may have been a considerable amount of 'catholic' art produced which has since been lost – or perhaps only mislaid.

5. J.M. Montias, 'Estimates of the Number of Dutch Master-Painters, their earnings and their output in 1650', *Leidschrift*, 6–3 (1990), 59–74; A.M. van der Woude, 'The volume and value of paintings in Holland at the time of the Dutch Republic', in David Freedberg and Jan de Vries (eds), *Art in History/History in Art. Studies in Seventeenth-Century Dutch Culture* (Santa Monica, CA, 1992).

6. J.M. Montias, *Artists and Artisans in Delft* (Princeton, NJ, 1982), pp. 117–18, 160–9.

7. For, perhaps, an extreme example, see S. Alpers, *Rembrandt's Enterprise. The Studio and the Market* (London, 1988).

8. As I tended to do in *Culture and Society*, ch. 6.

9. Evert M. Wiskerke, *De waardering voor de zeventiende-eeuws literatuur tussen 1780 en 1813* (Hilversum, 1995).

10. Pieter Cornelisz Hooft (1581–1647) lyric poet, playwright and historian.

11. Constantijn Huyghens (1596–1687) poet (and secretary to successive princes of Orange).

12. Joost van den Vondel (1587–1679) poet and dramatist.

13. Jacob Cats (1577–1660) poet (and also pensionary of Dordrecht and later *raadpensionaris*).

14. Gerbrand Adriaensz Bredero (1585–1618) poet and playwright.

15. In his own introduction to the *Tractatus theologico-politicus*.

16. S. Groenveld, 'The Mecca of Authors? States Assemblies and Censorship in the Seventeenth-Century Dutch Republic', *Too Mighty to be Free: Censorship and the Press in Britain and the Netherlands*, ed. A.C. Duke and C.A. Tamse (Zutphen, 1987), pp. 63–86.

17. Cf. K. van Berkel, 'From Simon Stevin to Robert Boyle: Reflections on the Place of Science in Dutch Culture in the Seventeenth Century', in *The Exchange of Ideas*, ed. Simon Groenveld and Michael Wintle (Zutphen, 1994), pp. 100–14.

18. J.I. Israel, 'Toleration in Seventeenth-Century Dutch and English Thought', in *The Exchange of Ideas*, pp. 13–30.

19. Cf. E. O. G. Haitsma Mulier, *The Myth of Venice and Dutch Republican Thought in the Seventeenth Century* (Assen, 1980).

20. Ibid., pp. 175–6.

21. Cf. J. Q. C. Mackrell, *The Attack on 'Feudalism' in Eighteenth-Century France* (London, 1973).

22. See, for example, G. C. J. J. van den Bergh: *The Life and Work of Gerardt Noodt (1647–1725). Dutch Legal Scholarship between Humanism and Enlightenment* (Oxford, 1988).

23. Cf. Pieter Spierenburg, *The Broken Spell: a Cultural and Anthropological History of Pre-industrial Europe* (Basingstoke, 1991).

24. See, most recently, Stuart Clark, *Thinking with Demons: the Idea of Witchcraft in Early Modern Europe* (Oxford, 1997).

25. See Johannes Hendrik Marie de Waardt, *Toverij en samenleving. Holland 1500–1800* (The Hague, 1991). A check-list of witchcraft prosecutions is to be found in Willem Frijhoff and Marijke Gijswijt-Hofstra, *Nederland betoverd* (Amsterdam, 1987), pp. 332ff.

26. Herman Roodenburg, *Onder censuur. De kerkelijke tucht in de Gereformeerde gemeente van Amsterdam, 1578–1700* (Hilversum, 1990).

27. Willem de Blécourt, *Termen van toverij. De veranderende betekenis van toverij in Noord-Oost Nederland tussen de 16de en 20ste eeuw* (Nijmegen, 1990).

28. This was first established for France in R. Mandrou, *Magistrats et sorciers en France au XVIIe siècle* (Paris, 1968); a similar argument with regard to the ending of such prosecutions in England is advanced in James Sharpe, *Instruments of Darkness. Witchcraft in England 1550–1750* (London, 1996), ch. 9.

29. Willem Frijhoff, *La société néerlandaise et ses gradués 1574–1784* (Amsterdam, 1981), p. 288.

30. Cf. J. L. Price, 'Regional identity and European culture: the North Sea region in the Early Modern Period', in Juliette Roding and Lex Heerma van Voss (eds), *The North Sea and Culture (1550–1800)* (Hilversum, 1996), pp. 78–95.

GLOSSARY

Advocaat van den Lande: legal adviser to the States of Holland; in the course of the Revolt it became the most important political office in the province. The office was abolished after the fall of Oldenbarnevelt, and replaced by that of *raadpensionaris*, see below.

arminian: follower of Jacobus Arminius, professor of theology at Leiden, who questioned conventional calvinist teachings, especially with regard to predestination.

buiten: a country house for town dwellers (lit. outside).

burgemeester: one of the leaders of a town's government; in Holland, towns usually had four burgemeesters.

contraremonstrant: opponent of the remonstrants, see below.

Council of State (*Raad van State*): effectively an executive committee of the States General with special responsibility for military affairs, the Generality lands, and other matters.

erasmian: undogmatic and ecumenical attitude to religion in the tradition of Erasmus.

Generality lands: areas (principally States Flanders and North Brabant) within the Republic, but outside the seven provinces represented in the States General.

gomarist: orthodox calvinist opponent of the arminians, named after the Leiden theologian, Franciscus Gomarus.

gracht: canal or street beside a canal.

Grote Vergadering (1651): emergency meeting of the provinces after the sudden death of Willem II.

mennonite: baptist sect of a pronounced pacifist character; named after their founder Menno Simons.

nadere reformatie: movement for a further reformation in the Reformed Church and Dutch society.

New Netherland: Dutch colony in North America; ceded to England after the Second Anglo-Dutch war and renamed New York.

pensionaris: in origin a salaried legal adviser, became one of the most important offices in town government.

raadpensionaris: grand pensionary, replacing the *Advocaat van den Lande*, see above; although a salaried office, it remained potentially the most powerful political post in Holland.

rasphuis: a house of correction with hard labour.

regeringsreglementen: changes to the political systems in the land provinces introduced under Willem III and designed to enhance his authority.

remonstrant: arminian, named after the Remonstrance presented to the States of Holland in 1610.

ridderschap: a body representing the nobility in many of the provincial states; membership did not include all of the nobles, but was restricted in various ways from province to province.

schepen: a town magistrate, member of the local court of justice and with considerable administrative responsibilities.

schuilkerken: literally, hidden churches, where catholics could meet for discreet worship.

schutter: member of *schutterij*.

schutterij: urban militia; service was a duty of citizens (thus also known as *burgerij*).

Sound Toll: duties levied by Denmark on ships entering and leaving the Baltic; they provide an invaluable record of trade during the early modern period.

stadhouder: governor of a province before the Revolt, the office retained most of its powers under the Republic.

States: representative bodies in the provinces, dominant politically under the Republic; membership mostly composed of towns and nobles in various combinations.

States General: the chief organ of central government, consisting of delegations from the states of each of the seven provinces of the Republic.

VOC (*Verenigde Oost-indische Compagnie*): Dutch East India Company.

wetsverzettingen: enforced changes in the personnel of town governments, usually by the stadhouder.

WIC: Dutch West India Company.

FURTHER READING

Svetlana Alpers, *The Art of Describing. Dutch Art in the Seventeenth Century* (London, 1983). Controversial but stimulating reinterpretation.

V. Barbour, *Capitalism in Amsterdam* (Baltimore, MD, 1950). Still a classic study.

C.R. Boxer, *The Dutch Seaborne Empire* (London, 1965). The best introduction to the subject in English.

Christopher Brown, *Scenes of Everyday Life. Dutch Genre Painting of the Seventeenth Century* (London, 1984). A judicious and penetrating discussion.

J.R. Bruijn, *The Dutch Navy in the Seventeenth and Eighteenth Centuries* (Colombia, SC, 1993). An excellent, short account.

Karel Davids and Jan Lucassen, *A Miracle Mirrored. The Dutch Republic in European Perspective* (Cambridge, 1995). A valuable collection.

Karel Davids and Leo Noordegraaf (eds), *The Dutch Economy in the Golden Age. Nine Studies* (Amsterdam, 1993). A good introduction to recent work on the Dutch economy.

A. Th. van Deursen, *Plain Lives in a Golden Age. Popular Culture, Religion and Society in Seventeenth-century Holland* (Cambridge, 1991). Essential reading.

Florike Egmond, *Underworlds. Organized Crime in the Netherlands 1650–1800* (Cambridge, 1993). A fascinating study of criminal bands, though weighted rather to the eighteenth century.

David Freedberg and Jan de Vries (eds), *Art in History / History in Art. Studies in Seventeenth-Century Dutch Culture* (Santa Monica, CA, 1992). Variable in quality but with important individual contributions.

Andrew C. Fix, *Prophecy and Reason. The Dutch Collegiants in the Early Enlightenment* (Princeton, NJ, 1991). Rather narrow in focus, but the best study available in English.

P. Geyl, *Orange and Stuart* (London, 1969). Originally published in 1939 and rather one-sided but still worth reading.

Pieter Geyl, *The Netherlands in the Seventeenth Century*, 2 vols (London 1961–4). Deals with both North and South, losing some coherence in the process; outdated in parts but still the work of a major historian.

M. Gijswijt-Hofstra and W. Frijhoff (eds), *Witchcraft in the Netherlands: From the Fourteenth to the Twentieth Century* (Rotterdam, 1991). Valuable collection of studies, much of it relevant to the seventeenth century.

B. Haak, *The Golden Age: Dutch Painters of the Seventeenth Century* (London, 1984). A useful, recent survey.

165

E.O.G. Haitsma Mulier, *The Myth of Venice and Dutch Republican Thought in the Seventeenth Century* (Assen, 1980). Introduces important themes in Dutch political thought.

K.H.D. Haley, *The Dutch in the Seventeenth Century* (London, 1972). A brief and sound introduction.

M. 't Hart, *The Making of a Bourgeois State. War, Politics and Finance during the Dutch Revolt* (Manchester, 1993). An important study, with the emphasis on the first half of the seventeenth century.

Johan Huizinga, *Dutch Civilisation in the Seventeenth Century* (London, 1968). Written in the 1930s and very much of its time, but essential reading.

J.I. Israel, *The Dutch Republic and the Hispanic World 1606–1661* (Oxford, 1982). A good account of this vital aspect of the Dutch international situation.

J.I. Israel, *Dutch Primacy in World Trade* (Oxford, 1989). Overschematic, contentious and indispensable.

J.I. Israel, 'Toleration in Seventeenth-Century Dutch and English Thought', in *The Exchange of Ideas*, ed. Simon Groenveld and Michael Wintle (Zutphen, 1994), pp. 13–30. Sees the theories of toleration springing from the remonstrants after their defeat.

Jonathan I. Israel, *The Dutch Republic. Its Rise, Greatness, and Fall 1477–1806* (Oxford, 1995). A major work.

J.R. Jones, *The Anglo-Dutch Wars of the Seventeenth Century* (London, 1996). Now the best work on the subject.

B.J. Kaplan: *Calvinists and Libertines. Confession and Community in Utrecht 1578–1620* (Oxford, 1995). Mainly on the late sixteenth century but important for the background to the religious crisis of the early seventeenth century.

Els Kloek, Nicole Teeuwen and Marijke Huisman (eds), *Women of the Golden Age. An International Debate on Women in Seventeenth-century Holland, England and Italy* (Hilversum, 1994). Includes interesting contributions on the situation in the Republic.

J.M. Montias, *Artists and Artisans in Delft* (Princeton, NJ, 1982). A fascinating study from an economist's point of view.

O. Mörke, 'Sovereignty and Authority. The role of the court in the Netherlands in the first half of the seventeenth century', in Ronald G. Asch and Adolf M. Birke (eds), *Princes, Patronage, and the Nobility. The Court at the Beginning of the Modern Age (c. 1450–1650)* (Oxford, 1991), pp. 455–77. Perhaps overstates his case, but worth reading.

H.F.K. van Nierop, *The Nobility of Holland. From Knights to Regents, 1500–1650* (Cambridge, 1993). An innovatory work which is essential reading.

D. Nobbs, *Theocracy and Toleration. A Study of the Disputes in Dutch Calvinism 1600–1650* (Cambridge, 1938). Despite its age, still the best account in English.

J.L. Price, *Culture and Society in the Dutch Republic during the Seventeenth Century* (London, 1974). The central argument seems perhaps a little simplistic now, but it remains a useful starting point.

J.L. Price, 'A State Dedicated to War? The Dutch Republic in the Seventeenth Century', in *The Medieval Military Revolution*, ed. Andrew Ayton and J.L. Price (London, 1995), pp. 183–200. A discussion of the peculiar nature of the Dutch state seen in relation to the demands of war.

J.L. Price, 'The Dutch Nobility in the Seventeenth and Eighteenth Centuries', in *The European Nobilities in the Seventeenth and Eighteenth Centuries*, vol. 1: *Western Europe*, ed. H.M. Scott (London, 1995). The best – the only – survey of the subject in English.

J.L. Price, *Holland and the Dutch Republic in the Seventeenth Century* (Oxford, 1994). Examines politics in Holland on three levels: town, province, and in relation to the government of the Republic.

Sir William Temple, *Observations upon the United Provinces of the Netherlands*, ed. Sir George Clark (Oxford, 1972). The work of an English ambassador to the Republic, of great interest both for the insights and for the misapprehensions.

Herbert H. Rowen, *Johan de Witt: Grand Pensionary of Holland* (Princeton, NJ, 1978). A large-scale narrative, interspersed with analytical chapters.

Herbert H. Rowen, *John de Witt. Statesman of the 'True Freedom'* (Cambridge, 1986). A much briefer introduction.

Herbert H. Rowen, *The Princes of Orange. The Stadholders in the Dutch Republic* (Cambridge, 1988). A collection of lively and readable studies.

G.V. Scammell, *The World Encompassed. The First European Maritime Empires* (London, 1981). His chapter on the Dutch provides the best short survey of the subject.

Simon Schama, *An Embarrassment of Riches. An Interpretation of Dutch Culture in the Golden Age* (London, 1987). Prolix and idiosyncratic; to be read with caution.

M.A. Schenkeveld, *Dutch Literature in the Age of Rembrandt* (Amsterdam, 1991). A readable survey; the best introduction in English.

Jan de Tex, *Oldenbarnevelt*, 2 vols (Cambridge, 1973). Necessary reading for the religious and political crisis of the early seventeenth century.

Jan de Vries and Ad van der Woude, *The First Modern Economy. Success, Failure, and Perseverance of the Dutch Economy, 1500–1815* (Cambridge, 1997). A magisterial analysis.

Jan de Vries, *The Dutch Rural Economy in the Golden Age 1500–1700* (New Haven, CT, 1974). A pioneering work, still very useful.

Jan de Vries, *Barges and Capitalism. Passenger Transportation in the Dutch Economy (1632–1839)* (Wageningen, 1978). Considerably more interesting, and important, than the title might suggest.

J.L. van Zanden, *The Rise and Decline of Holland's Economy. Merchant Capitalism and the Labour Market* (Manchester, 1993). A challenging new interpretation.

INDEX

admiralties 32–3
Alkmaar 102
Amboina 36
Ames, William 101
Amsterdam 19, 29, 41, 45, 46, 47, 56, 57, 71, 72, 85, 92, 97, 103, 111, 114, 115, 116, 117, 120
anabaptists 6
Anglo-Dutch wars 26, 32, 37, 55, 118
anticlericalism 7
Antwerp 3, 10, 20, 54, 60
Aragon 18
Arminius, Jacobus 101
army 20, 31–2, 75, 118; military reforms 12
art 130, 131–4
Australia 37
Austrian Habsburgs 24, 27, 30

Banda Islands 21
Batavia 59
Bayle, Pierre 139
Bekker, Balthasar 99, 105, 106, 149
Bohemian revolt 24, 34
Bordeaux 47
Bourignon, Antoinette 97
Brabant 2, 3, 42, 84; States (North) Brabant 4, 19, 40, 41, 84, 93, 96, 112, 119, 120, 148
Brazil 21, 26, 36, 58
Breda 28
Bredero, Gerbrand Adriaensz 136
Bruges 60

Cape of Good Hope 57, 58
Castille 18

Catalonia 18, 23, 28
Catholic Church 13, 24, 89, 93, 94, 140
Catholic League 2, 10
catholics 5, 7, 87, 93–6, 140
Cats, Jacob 135, 136
Charles I, king of England 30
Charles II, king of England 27, 30
Charles V, Holy Roman emperor 3, 17
China 37
classical studies 129
Clerc, Jean le 97
Cocceius, Johannes 99
Cockayne project (1614) 54
Colbert, Jean-Baptiste 53, 54
collegiants 97
Cologne 48, 94
colonial expansion 19, 20–1, 35–6
Counter-Reformation 7, 24, 25
Court, Johan de la 141–2
Court, Pieter de la 141–2
Curaçao 58

Danzig 46, 53
Delft 41, 54, 114
Denmark 16, 20
De Rijp 110, 112
Descartes, René 99, 137
Deventer 68, 120
Devolution, War of (1666–7) 23, 27, 37
dissenters 6, 96–9
Dordrecht 91, 114
Dordt (Dordrecht), synod of 91, 92, 104
Dou, Gerrit 133

Drenthe 84, 111, 119, 125
Dunkirk 47

East Friesland 84
economy ch. 2 *passim*, 50, 55–6,
  59–60; agriculture 9, 42, 44,
  51–2; Baltic trade 8, 40, 42, 44,
  46, 51, 55; finance 56–7;
  fishing 8, 26–7, 40, 43, 44, 45,
  47–8, 118; decline 42;
  growth 7–8, 39–40, 45–6, 52–4,
  108–9; infrastructure 49–50;
  manufactures 43–4, 48–9;
  merchant fleet 26, 45, 47, 55,
  117–18; textile industry 8, 43,
  45, 48, 49; trade 19, 46–7;
  shipbuilding 43, 48–9;
  trafieken 49
education 116–17, 144–5
Eighty Years War 22–3, 37
Elizabeth I, queen of England 10,
  16
England 10, 22, 25, 26, 27, 34, 38,
  47, 52, 54, 65
Enkhuizen 114, 115
Episcopius (Bischop), Simon 97

Farnesa, Alexander *see* Parma
Ferdinand, king of Aragon 17
Flanders 2, 3, 20, 42, 84
foreign policy ch. 1 *passim*, 28–9,
  65; England 26, 27, 30, 31;
  France 27, 28, 29, 34–5;
  Jülich-Kleve 20; religion 25,
  30, 31, 33; southern Netherlands
  19, 28–9; Spain 28, 33–4; Triple
  Alliance 37
France 2, 10, 22, 23, 24, 25, 27,
  34, 37, 46, 53; French tariffs 54
Franche-Comté 23
Franeker, university of 116
Frederik Hendrik, prince of
  Orange 21, 29, 70, 74, 75, 76, 104
Friesland 3, 4, 50, 68–9, 78, 80,
  90, 111, 118, 125, 147

Galileo 138
Geer, Louis de 116

Gelderland 3, 4, 40, 68, 75, 78, 80,
  84, 93, 119, 120, 125, 126, 148
Generality lands 66, 84, 90, 93,
  94
Geneva 17
Geyl, Pieter 14, 84
Ghent 60
Gomarus, Franciscus 101
Gouda 41, 43, 54
Graft 112
Groningen (province) 3, 50, 68,
  69, 80, 119, 125, 148
Groningen (town) 3, 68;
  university 116
Grotius, Hugo 140, 141
Gustavus Adolphus, king of
  Sweden 17, 34

Haarlem 8, 41, 43, 45, 48, 49, 54,
  56, 87, 114, 115, 117
Hague, The 41, 114, 115
Haley, K.H.D. 14
Hals, Frans 133
Hanover 38
Harderwijk, university of 116
Henri III, king of France 16
Henry IV, king of France 10, 11,
  25, 30
Holy Roman Empire 24, 25, 28,
  34, 53, 65
Holland 1, 2, 3, 4, 8–9, 12, 14, 22,
  29–30, 50, 66–7, 75, 76, 80, 84–5,
  90, 91, 94, 96, 105, 119, 147–8,
  149; civic militias 72; Court of
  Holland (*Hof*) 72;
  economy 39–40, 42, 44, 47,
  50–1, 59–60, 110, 111;
  gecommitteerde raden 79; High
  Council (*Hoge Raad*) 72;
  nobles 71, 75, 126; political
  system 69–72, 78;
  population 40–1, 78; States
  of 12, 63–4, 68, 79, 102;
  towns 8, 16, 50, 51, 63, 68, 71,
  72, 75, 79, 109, 113–14, 122
Hooft, Pieter Cornelisz 135, 136
Hoorn 48, 114, 115
Huygens, Christiaen 138

Huygens, Constantijn 135, 136

India 35
Indonesia 59
Isabella, queen of Castille 17
Israel, Jonathan 14
Israel, Menasseh ben 100
Italy 53

James I, king of England 10
James II, king of England 27
Japan 58
Java 20, 21, 36, 37, 57, 58
jews 99–100

Kampen 68, 120
Koerbagh, Adriaen 138

Labadie, Jean de 97
law 129, 145
Leeuwenhoek, Anthonie van 139
Leicester, Robert Dudley, earl of 4, 16, 70
Leiden 8, 41, 45, 48, 49, 54, 56, 71, 114, 115, 117; university 102, 116, 129
Limburg 19
literature 130, 134–7
Louis XIV, king of France 31, 34
Low Countries 1, 60
Luzac, Elie 62

Maas, river 43
Malaysia 58
Maurits, count of Nassau, later prince of Orange 12, 21, 66–7, 70, 73, 74, 75, 76, 77, 81, 82, 85, 101, 103
medicine 129, 145
mennonites 6, 87, 97–8
Merchant Adventurers 54
Mexico 10, 23
Milan 23
Moluccas 20, 58
Monnikendam 71
Münster, bishop of 26
Münster, treaty of (1648) 23, 31, 66

Nantes 47
Naples 23
navy 12, 32–3
Netherlands, Kingdom of the 1, 61
Netherlands, Revolt of 1, 5, 7, 24, 77; privileges 4, 81; religion 24, 96
New Netherland 57, 58, 99
Nine Years War 118
Noodt, Gerard 145
Norway 48, 122

Oldenbarnevelt, Johan van 11, 16, 21, 25, 70, 71, 72, 73, 74, 76, 85, 101, 103
Orange, princes of 21, 22, 28–9, 30, 61–2, 62–3, 68, 70, 73–7, 78, 85, 132
orangism 67, 68, 77, 80, 82–3
Ottoman empire 10, 18
Overijssel 3, 40, 68, 75, 80, 94, 119, 120, 125

Pacification of Ghent (1576) 1, 3, 16
Parma, Alexander Farnesa, prince of 2, 10, 11, 33
Peru 10, 23
Philip II, king of Spain 2, 10, 11, 16
philosophy 130
Plockhoy, Pieter 99
political system ch. 3 *passim*, 64–5, 65–7, 69–70; Council of State 71, 75–6; decentralisation 21; *Grote Vergadering* 67; provincial states 63, 64, 66–7; *regeringsreglementen* 76; stadhoudership 63, 74, 75, 78–9; States General 2, 4, 20, 63, 66, 69, 70
population 40
Portugal 10, 17, 18, 23, 26, 28
puritanism 92
Purmerend 71

Reformed Church 5–6, 7, 13, 30, 63, 76, 77, 82–3, 87, 89–93, 95,

104; *nadere reformatie* 92–3, 99, 143

regents 6, 29, 30, 37, 64, 68, 77–80, 82, 83, 87–88, 90–1, 102, 106, 126–7, 146

religious toleration 86–9, 106–7, 140, 143

Rembrandt van Rijn 129, 132

remonstrants 13, 81, 83, 92, 97

remonstrant/contraremonstrant conflict 100–4

republicanism 63–4, 80; political theory 62, 81–2, 141–2; system of government 21–2

Rijnsburg 97

Rotterdam 12, 41, 47, 71, 114, 116

Salmasius, Claude 141

Schelde, blockade of 19, 56

Schurman, Anna Maria van 99

science 130, 138–9

Scotland 48

Sicily 23

Smith, Adam 46

society ch. 5 *passim*; *burgerij* 109–10; land provinces 119–21; nobles 62, 68, 79–80, 124–7; rural change 110–13; urban change 113–21; women 121–4

Sound Toll 20

Spain 1, 9, 10, 17–18, 22, 23, 46, 53; Spanish Armada 2, 11; army in the Netherlands 2, 10–11, 33; Spanish rule in the Netherlands 3, 4, 11, 23, 28, 88; Baltic plans 24

Spanish Netherlands 49, 56

Spinoza, Benedict de 137, 142

Sri Lanka 21, 36, 37, 57, 58, 59

States General *see* political system

Stevin, Simon 138

Surinam 58

Sweden 17, 20, 28

Swiss Confederation 17, 65

Taiwan 58

Teellinck, Willem 92

Temple, Sir William 62–3, 65

theology 129, 140

Thirty Years War 17, 23, 24, 28, 34, 37, 55

Trip family 116

Twelve Years Truce (1609) 2, 9, 12, 22, 26, 28, 31; internal problems during 13, 30, 95, 103–4; negotiations for 13–14, 16

Twente 41, 112, 120

urbanisation 42, 60, 113–14

Utrecht (province) 3, 40, 75, 80, 94, 119, 125

Utrecht, treaty of (1713) 18

Utrecht, Union of (1579) 2, 16

Utrecht, university of 92, 116

Velázquez, Diego 28

Veluwe 41

Venice 34

VOC (*Vereenigde Oostindische Compagnie*) 20–1, 35–6, 57, 58, 59, 118

Voetius (Voet), Gijsbert 92

Vondel, Joost van den 135, 144

Westphalia, Peace of 24

WIC (*Westindische Compagnie*) 21, 26, 35–6, 57, 58, 59, 103

Wier, Johan 149

William the Silent *see* Willem I

Willem I, prince of Orange 10, 63, 73, 76–7, 81

Willem II, prince of Orange 21, 29, 67, 70, 71, 74, 75, 81

Willem III, prince of Orange, later king of England 21, 27, 29, 32, 34, 70, 74, 75, 76, 81

Willem Lodewijk, count of Nassau 12

witchcraft 104–6, 146–9

Witt, Johan de 32, 65, 70, 71, 74

Zaandam 55

Zaanstreek 49, 50–1, 54, 112, 115, 118

Zeeland   1, 3, 4, 16, 42, 50, 75, 78,
    80, 90, 105, 111, 118, 119, 147;
    First Noble   75; States of   66
Zürich   17

Zuider Zee   43, 50
Zwammerdam, Jan   99
Zwolle   68, 120